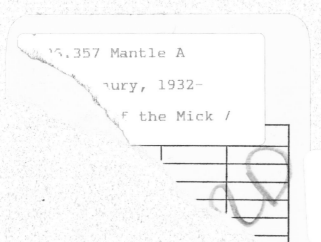

Memories of the Mick

Memories of
THE Mick

MAURY ALLEN

Photos by **Bob Olen**

Introduction by **David Halberstam**

Taylor Publishing Company

Dallas, Texas

Published by Taylor Publishing Company
        1550 West Mockingbird Lane
        Dallas, TX 75235

Allen, Maury,   1932–
        Memories of the Mick / Maury Allen; photos by Bob Olen; introduction by David Halberstam.
            p.   cm.
        Includes index.
        ISBN 0-87833-958-2
        1. Mantle, Mickey, 1931–   . 2. Baseball players—United States—Biography.
    3. New York Yankees (Baseball team)—History.
    I. Title.
    GV865.M33A45   1997
    796.357'092—dc21
    [B]   96-54060
                                                                                                              CIP

Printed in the United States of America

10   9   8   7   6   5   4   3   2   1

Contents

Memories of the Mick

Introduction

BY DAVID HALBERSTAM

No one is better qualified to write about Mickey Mantle than Maury Allen. Allen was one of the original "chipmunks," a name given to a handful of young, talented, and irreverent sportswriters who came to prominence in New York in the late fifties and early sixties, and who decided to write about athletes more as they really were and, in the words of the great Red Smith (a chipmunk before there were chipmunks), stop "godding" them up for their readers.

The chipmunks were bright, talented, iconoclastic, and they thought that their readers were entitled to see the world of sports with some degree of honesty. There was a generational fault line between them and those who went before them, those who had taken the athletes at face value, erased their warts, and effectively airbrushed portraits of them. The *New York Post*, the paper for which Allen worked, was a major center of chipmunk journalism; it was in those days a lively, well-written liberal paper and a pleasurable antidote to the heavier sports pages of the *Times*, where there was a deadly, joyless quality to much of the sportswriting.

Allen, who grew up as a New York City anomaly—a Brooklyn kid who loved the Yankees—started covering the Yankees in 1959. He was just twenty-seven at the time. He brought with him a high degree of professionalism, a desire to be part of the journalistic changes then beginning to sweep city rooms and sports desks throughout the country, and that meant he was destined for an inevitable collision with Mantle, the signature Yankee star of the era.

Mantle, something of a mensch at the end of his life and at the end of his career, was in fact a player who for much of his career was uncomfortable playing, not just in a big city that was the media capital of the world, but playing in the shadow of the great DiMaggio. DiMaggio had not only been the signature figure of the great Yankees teams of the past, but he had received adulatory treatment by members of the adoring and significantly less irreverent preceding generation of New York sportswriters. (Having been told by their elders that DiMaggio was, not only the most gifted baseball player of a generation, but a wonderful human being as well, Allen and a number of his colleagues were surprised to find that the DiMaggio they dealt with, even when his career was over and he should have been relaxed, was a somewhat suspicious, not particularly generous man who was quick to cut off any writer who did not seem properly reverential.)

The Mantle whom Allen found was a country boy still trying to come to terms with his role as superstar in the big city, a gifted, moody player uncomfortable with the burden of fame and the pressure inherent in the role as the Yankee superstar in an era when the Yankees were expected to win every year. More than any athlete of his era, he was burdened by expectations, those of his father at first; then of his manager, Casey Stengel; and finally of his fans. No matter what he did, it was never good enough; no matter how well he hit, he should have hit 30 points higher.

For Mantle the city itself was threatening. Brought to New York as a teenager, he had never entirely grown up. The city made him ill at ease, and he took out his release in late-night carousing. He was, quite predictably, good with his teammates, who were almost all country boys and who understood the burdens he carried, and bad with the media representatives, who were all city boys and who seemed in his eyes (as it always is with athletes) to concentrate not on what he did right on a given day but on what he had done wrong. Mantle and Allen represented two age-old cultures which have never meshed particularly well and which are almost always in collision.

The young Mantle had a hard time with the young Maury Allen, who was very good at what he did. I was once a reporter in Vietnam, but it should be said that those few pioneer sportswriters who brought a greater degree of candor to the nation's sports page had every bit as much integrity as the reporters who began to challenge the official government line in Saigon at much the same time. There was nothing easy or pleasant about going to a locker room every day where powerful, muscular, much-adored young men tended to see you as the villain and treat you as an outcast. The Mantle-Allen relationship was for a number of years a rocky one. A semifamous moment occurred when Allen was watching Mantle take pregame swings one day. Mantle looked over at him and said, in a not very pleasant voice, "You piss me off just standing there." It should be noted that phrase became something of a slogan in the Allen household, and various Allen family members used it in addressing each other in succeeding weeks and months.

In time, after Roger Maris's victory in the 1961 home run derby when the traditional Yankee fans belatedly decided the competition was no longer between Mantle and DiMaggio but between Mantle and Maris, the fans finally began to accept Mantle. ("Roger has stolen my fans," Mantle said with no small amount of irony, meaning that the boo birds who once belonged to him were now working on Maris.) Suddenly much of the burden on Mantle's shoulders seemed to be lifted. He mellowed considerably and began to treat Maury Allen and other writers better, as well he should.

Maury Allen is an accomplished professional, and I'm proud to call him my friend.

One Last Time

There were *fifteen hundred dreamers in that large ball-room of the Sheraton New York Hotel on January 22, 1995. They were mostly men in their fifties and sixties, fathers and sons, old pals, business associates, fans, followers, all emotionally linked to each other and to the game of baseball.*

It had been a vicious winter season for many of them. They had grown bitter over the endless labor disputes in the game. Play had been cut off on August 12 the year before, depriving them of the passion of a World Series.

On this evening, the audience had put aside the routine of their lives, their schedules and tensions. Baseball always seemed to soften their anger and warm their spirit. It made their own lives seem less pedestrian.

Many of them had sat in this same ballroom many January nights as the New York chapter of the Baseball Writers Association of America paraded the joys of their youth before them.

The dinner had gone on for seventy-two years by now, started as an excuse to entertain and honor baseball players during the winter, and to stimulate baseball conversation. The sportswriters had honored dozens of legendary figures in the game through the decades. There were presentations to Babe Ruth, Lou Gehrig, Ty Cobb, Joe DiMaggio, Casey Stengel, Ted Williams, Bob Feller, Stan Musial, Sandy Koufax, and many more.

When it was time to sell out that huge ballroom again, the accomplished stars of the aborted 1994 season, Frank Thomas, Jeff Bagwell, Greg Maddux, would not achieve that goal.

There had always been a mixture of stars at this dinner—the greats of the past and the heroes of the present. An aging Ruth sitting next to a young DiMaggio. A rambunctious Stengel bending the ear of his young creation, Billy Martin. An ailing Sal Maglie with a shy Sandy Koufax.

The sportswriters had to save the 1995 dinner and maintain the tradition with a perfect dais of honorees.

"Willie, Mickey and the Duke" rang in so many heads, as they had in the spilling of names from composer Terry Cashman's pen when he wrote a lyrical number called, "Talkin' Baseball."

Never before and never again would New York see the excellence, elegance, and energy manifested by the play of these three New York baseball icons. These three center fielders were the young lions, the folk figures from the years 1951 through 1957.

Duke Snider had been a Brooklyn Dodgers center fielder since 1947. Two other youngsters would rival him for acclaim in 1951. One, a blue-eyed, blond, crew-cut 18-year-old boy from Oklahoma, had joined the Yankees from his farm club in Joplin, Missouri, in the final days of the 1950 season. The other had joined the Giants from his farm club at Minneapolis in the last days of May 1951.

The first youngster would make the team in the spring of 1951 and play right field next to the great DiMaggio on opening day. The other would make the team as soon as he arrived in May despite starting off without a hit in three straight games.

Willie Mays, the center fielder of the New York Giants, was soon being called the "Say Hey Kid" in the press. He addressed everyone with the call of "say, hey," whenever the other person's name slipped his mind.

The Yankee youngster could hardly address a stranger. He could hardly address a teammate. He was still eighteen when he joined the Yankees on the road in 1950 and barely past his nineteenth birthday when he first arrived in New York in 1951.

Mickey Mantle.

His father, Elvin "Mutt" Mantle, had given him that resonant name when he was born October 20, 1931, in Spavinaw, Oklahoma. Mutt Mantle had admired Detroit catcher Mickey Cochrane and wanted his own son to be a player of the same category.

Mickey Mantle.

"I don't think that my father ever knew that Mickey Cochrane's real first name was Gordon," Mantle would say in his 1974 Hall of Fame induction speech. "I hope there's no Gordons here today, but I'm glad that he didn't name me Gordon."

Gordon Mantle?

For the 1995 dinner, wise heads among the sportswriters brainstormed a marvelous solution. They would present an award named the Willie, Mickey and the Duke Award to these three men and forever after to special honorees of the past who could honorably carry their tradition forward.

Snider was easy to reach. He loved coming back to New York for any excuse. He had won Hall of Fame honors for his play in Brooklyn and in Los Angeles with the Dodgers. He had even taken a turn with the early New York Mets and finished up his career with the San Francisco Giants. He agreed to show up for the dinner.

Mays was more difficult. He was always a bit prickly on these issues, unsure if he cared to be seen in public, sensitive to what might be said or written of him. He was also anxious to know the details concerning accommodations and the conditions. If the other two showed, he agreed to come to the dinner.

Mickey Mantle.

He would be the challenge. After finally admitting a lifelong problem with alcohol, he had spent time at the Betty Ford Clinic and had gone on national television with sportscaster Bob Costas to admit his indiscretions, to cleanse his soul, to rebuild his aging life.

Mantle's father had died at the age of thirty-nine. Several of his uncles had also died at early ages. When Mantle reached his fiftieth birthday, an age no adult male in his immediate family had made it to, he began kidding about his longevity.

"If I had known I would live this long, I would have taken better care of myself," he would often say.

It was a joke line.

He never took good care of himself. He began drinking as a high-school kid. He accelerated as a minor-league professional player. He tried hard to keep up with the established stars as a Yankee and spent most of his after-career years at banquets, golf tournaments, and baseball card shows where drinking was de rigueur. It was the manly thing to do, the code of the road, the macho style of men in that athletic, fraternal, jovial group.

Some, like manager Casey Stengel, died at the age of eighty-five after a long life of drink.

Others, like Mantle, would not make it that far.

Still others, dry and sober all their lives, died at terribly young ages. Lou Gehrig, a prince of man with high moral standards, was dead at the age of thirty-seven. Who knew?

Mantle had been drinking heavily his last years. He had arrived at the 1988 New York Baseball Writers dinner in an inebriated state. He had come to receive the Joe DiMaggio Toast of the Town Award, honoring his Yankee predecessor. When it came time for him to accept the honor, he stumbled over some of his words, giggled embarrassingly at the microphone, and told a raunchy story about former Yankees general manager George Weiss.

Most of the audience only laughed. "That's Mick," many said. No one on the dais or in the audience would ever say, "The man needs help."

Five years later, moved by the advice of Pat Summerall, a former New York Giants kicker and old friend from the 1950s, Mantle had realized that he needed help.

Doctors had finally reached him after he blacked out on an airplane ride and was taken to a hospital for treatment. "They told me, 'Mick, if you don't stop drinking, you'll be dead.' I stopped. Just like that. I stopped," he said.

Now it was more than a year after the stay at Betty Ford, more than a year of soft drinks, more than a year of changing a life style he had enjoyed for over forty years.

Snider and Mays had settled into the VIP Princess Suite at the New York Sheraton Hotel. They sat quietly at separate small tables. Baseball players and officials, including the new presidents of the leagues, Leonard Coleman of the National League and Gene Budig of the American League, had walked up to them. Shyly they introduced themselves, and attempted small talk. In baseball's traditional, corporate fumbling ways, these two men had been named presidents of the leagues and nobody had ever heard of either of them at a ballpark. Their league publicist escorted them around the room. Snider and Mays hardly noticed.

The dinner was set to begin shortly after seven o'clock. Hundreds of people had already gathered at the ballroom entrance, moving forward anxiously, hoping for a glimpse of their heroes.

The noise level outside the entrance to the Princess Suite increased dramatically. Uniformed security guards opened the door. They waved their arms in the air as if to clear out any invisible interlopers. Suddenly, he was there.

Mickey Mantle.

He was wearing a tuxedo with the bow tie slightly askew. He carried a topcoat over his left arm. The coat was quickly retrieved by a security guard who placed it on a side rack. Mantle had a small smile on his face. His hair, slightly gray at the temples, was still dark at the center, almost reddish, with a wide part in front and a boyish wave on the side.

Mays got up from his seat and walked a few paces to greet him. They shook hands warmly, Mays pressing Mickey's right hand into both of his.

"I remember when we first came up," Mays would say several days after the dinner, "and people began writing about us as being the two best young center fielders in the game, creating some sort of rivalry. Mickey was in the other league. All I wanted to do was hit."

Mays hadn't hit at first and manager Leo Durocher, certain of Mays's skills, had reminded him that the job was his no matter what he did at the plate. He could field, he could run, and he could throw. The hitting would come, Durocher reminded the youngster.

There would be 660 home runs after he broke through with that first one off Warren Spahn, future Hall of Famer, who used to kid, "Nobody would have ever heard of Willie if I didn't give up that homer to him."

Soon Mantle and Mays were linked in the minds of the baseball fans, measured against each other for home runs and titles. They were paired as the best youngsters in the game, starting in 1954 when Mays returned from military service.

"We got very close in later years," Mays would say after that dinner. "We did a lot of card shows together. We helped each other make a lot of money. Actually they never would bring us to a card show on the same day. It would be too much. Either I signed or Mickey signed. That was always the way it was."

Now, on this January evening, they seemed exceptionally close, the white man from Oklahoma and the black man from Alabama, bonded together by performance and perception.

Snider, a little older than the other two at sixty-nine, would soon join them in the corner of the room. He shook hands warmly, chatted with both of them about being back in New York together for the first time at this dinner, and then placed a box of baseballs on the table. He had signed these balls himself and now he wanted Mantle and Mays to sign them for his own collection.

The signing of baseballs had become a ritual unlike any other in the life and times of famous baseball players. It would often be the first thing a ballplayer would do when he entered a clubhouse and the last thing he would do before he left.

Mays, Snider, and Mantle had each signed their names many thousands of times by now, and still it went on everywhere they went, with everyone they came across, at every public occasion of their lives. Each told stories about checks that went uncollected because the payees would rather save the autograph than turn their signatures into insignificant money.

At Mantle's funeral, Bob Costas, doing the eulogy, would tell a story Mickey loved to repeat at public events. It had so succinctly captured the autograph times.

"It brings to mind a story Mickey liked to tell on himself," Costas related at the podium of Lovers Lane United Methodist Church in Dallas, "and maybe some of you have heard it. He pictured himself at the pearly gates, met by St. Peter who shook his head and said, 'Mick, we checked the record. We know some of what went on. Sorry we can't let you in. But before you go, God wants to know if you'd sign these six dozen baseballs.'"

Mickey signed a few baseballs for Snider at the dinner. The autograph seemed steady, clean and clear— as exacting as it had been almost forty-five years ago when he sat on a train going to Washington, DC, to sign his first Yankee contract before a game against the Washington Senators.

The value of his autograph had grown enormously through the years. His 1952 baseball card was valued at anywhere from fifty to seventy thousand dollars to the right buyer—if his autograph was on the card.

"I really can't understand it," he told me one afternoon a few years earlier, as he sat at the back table of Mickey Mantle's, the restaurant on Central Park South in Manhattan, which carried his name forward for so many fans. "I sign my name and make more money in one day than I made in any one season I ever played for the Yankees. Too bad I didn't save all those old uniforms and undershirts that people wanted. How much would you pay for a signed jock?"

The signing of autographs had become a professional enterprise for Mantle, for Mays, and for Snider. They would receive huge sums from promoters for appearances at these autograph card shows. Sometimes it would cause problems. In 1995 Snider experienced federal tax evasion problems, which damaged his image and diminished his autograph's worth.

After they signed a few baseballs and a few books thrust at them in the Princess Suite, Mantle, Mays, and Snider began to move to the back wall. This would be the moment when photographers would capture them together.

They never really had been captured on film together before. Though each had been at this dinner several times, they had never been invited together because the sportswriters believed that would only overwhelm their audience and create hard feelings by those who had been denied tickets. Fire laws prevented more than fifteen hundred persons in the huge ballroom, and a public invitation featuring all three, in a year when current stars would also draw their share of fans, would be unthinkable.

In 1995 it had worked because so many fans were angry about the game. A strike and the loss of a World Series had shocked baseball fans. But Willie, Mickey, and the Duke had filled the room and saved the dinner.

Snider, with thinning silver hair, some extra weight around the middle, and a pair of thick glasses, stood alone against the back wall. He waited for Mays and Mantle to join him. Mays, slightly overweight, some lines deepened in his face, as animated as ever, joined Snider. These two were rivals, to be sure—one a hero of the Brooklyn Dodgers, the other a saint from the New York Giants.

The pain of the 1951 season, maybe the most famous in New York baseball history, was not discussed that day, but it could not have been too far back in the minds of each. The Brooklyn Dodgers had led the Giants 4-1 in the final 1951 playoff game at the Polo Grounds in Harlem. The Giants scored a run in the bottom of the ninth and had two runners on base when Ralph Branca relieved Don Newcombe for Brooklyn. Snider stood in center field as Branca passed him and said, "Go get 'em."

Bobby Thomson was the batter, and Mays, a rookie then, was the next hitter. Charlie Dressen, the Brooklyn manager, would not walk the lead run in Thompson and have Branca pitch to Mays with one out. Dressen felt Thomson, who had already homered off Branca, was an easier out than the young Mays.

"My knees were shaking as Bobby went to the plate," Mays would later say. "I kept praying he would hit it out so I didn't have to bat."

Thomson took a strike and hit the next pitch into the lower left-field stands for a three-run homer, a 5-4 New York Giants win, and the National League pennant.

"When I was running around the bases," Thomson would later say, "I wasn't thinking I had hit a homer that had won the pennant. I was thinking I had hit a homer that had beaten Brooklyn. That's what was on my mind, beating Brooklyn."

Durocher had managed Brooklyn until switching to the Giants in 1948. He had always emphasized that rivalry with his players. Beat Brooklyn. That seemed more important than life itself.

The Giants won that pennant in 1951 and faced the Yankees in the

World Series. Mickey had played two games as the rookie right fielder, then injured himself catching a ball by stepping in a drain. He would not play against a Mays team until the Giants were in San Francisco in 1962.

Rivalries abounded. The Yankees had tortured the Boston Red Sox ever since Babe Ruth moved from Boston to New York in 1920. The St. Louis Cardinals and the Chicago Cubs had fought over many pennants. The Cleveland Indians and the Detroit Tigers had battled for generations. Even the new Los Angeles Dodgers and the new San Francisco Giants, each born in 1958, had engaged in some fierce competition.

Those rivalries were all minor compared to Brooklyn and New York throughout the 1930s, 1940s, and the glorious years of the 1950s. From 1951 on, Mays and Snider had been the two center fielders most identified with the intensity of that rivalry.

Whatever the competition, whatever the rivalry, whatever the anger and anguish over so many playing years, all of that seems to disappear in middle age for most baseball players. They may have fought on the field in the prime of their youth. In the dwindling of their days, they are only connected.

To have played major league baseball, to have faced a fastball aimed at your head at one hundred miles an hour, to have lived through pennant triumphs and suffered wrenching defeat are emotions no others could understand.

Fans, friends, even sportswriters traveling the same avenues, staying at the same hotels, drinking at the same bars, could never identify with the inner sense of what it is really like to suit up for a big-league game.

The fraternity of players is like no other. No matter how much the game is loved by outsiders, it is only truly felt by the insiders.

Upon his retirement after the 1968 season, Mantle was asked what he missed most about not playing. Everyone expected his answer would revolve around a giant home run, a leaping catch, a victory in a World Series, or the sense of satisfaction in a job well done. It was none of these for Mickey.

"What I miss most," he said, "is not being in the clubhouse with the guys, not sharing the jokes, not being part of the team."

Maybe soldiers in a foxhole or pilots in a squadron or doctors around an operating table can feel that oneness. Sportswriters, bitter, jealous, egomaniacal sometimes, never have that sense of fraternity.

At the 1995 dinner, Bill Liederman, the man who owns Mickey Mantle's restaurant in Manhattan and a friend for several years, urged Mantle to the back of the room for the photo opportunity. Mantle got up slowly from his chair, walking with a slight limp to join the other two in front of the back wall.

They had now gathered for this historical moment.

Each seemed incredibly happy to pose for these pictures. They were clasping each other in a fraternal way, joining the bantering the photographers engaged in as they tried to lessen the pain of "just one more."

The three stood against that wall for ten or fifteen minutes. Hundreds of photos were taken, as if in some mystical way each photographer knew this opportunity would not present itself again.

There are complicated logistics involved in any gathering of sports heroes. It is difficult to blend their busy schedules, collect them at convenient times, and show them off at a special moment. Each of these photographers had been at dozens of similar events and always they would be one short at photo time—a last minute cancellation, a plane missed, a date forgotten, or a conflict of appointments. Never had these three been photographed together before.

Finally the photos were finished. They would be seen in newspapers the next day and remembered with pleasure when viewed in the following year's Baseball Writers dinner program. With the photo session over, other guests walked over to the three greats.

The league presidents, old sportswriters, and even working photographers wanted a picture with them. The younger stars of the game, being honored that night, also moved in range. These were the new heroes—Frank Thomas of the White Sox, Jeff Bagwell of the Astros, and Greg Maddux of the Braves.

All wanted to pose with the three legendary center fielders of New York for their own purposes, for their families, for their own connection with greatness.

It was nearly time to bring these three men out of the privacy of the Princess Suite and into the public arena of the Sheraton ballroom.

They were soon seated along a side wall. Each waited patiently as the other honorees of the night assumed their respective positions. The side door to the ballroom was opened. The eyes of the people in the audience, many of whom had attended this dinner twenty, thirty, or forty times, fixed on the dais guests.

The line of tuxedo-clad men all walked along a side wall of the ballroom now. They turned forward and moved to the dais in a prescribed order. League presidents, most valuable players, Cy Young Award winners, and batting champions flanked the three superstars at their center.

In the middle of the line, Mantle, Mays, and Snider reached their seats. The applause rose from the back of the ballroom, growing louder and louder as each of these three, heroes of a distant day, stood on the dais.

"Mickey, Mickey, Mickey," yelled several guests as Mantle stared straight ahead. This was not a time for a wave, a laugh, a kidding remark, or a gesture of recognition. This was a time to be part of a team.

The first introduction from Claire Smith, the chairperson of the Baseball Writers Association and a *New York Times* sportswriter, was for operatic star Arthur Rubin, who would sing the National Anthem. He moved to the microphone, waited his cue, and delivered the opening notes with a voice that filled the room and stilled the audience.

Smith then told the eager audience that dinner was now served and that the festivities they were waiting for were an hour or so away.

Mantle sat next to Mays and Snider, and the three of them engaged in kidding conversation about their increased girth, their decreased hair and their joy at being together at this event.

Mays asked Mantle about his health after his stay at Betty Ford and the recurring newspaper reports about blackouts, stomach problems, and shortness of breath.

"I feel good. I really feel good," Mickey told Mays. "I probably should have done this a long time ago, but I'm glad I finally did. The doctors say I can live a long, healthy life now. I hope so."

Both Snider and Mays, each of whom had some difficult days with their own health, congratulated Mickey on his willpower.

"It was a tough time when I was in there," Mantle said of the Betty Ford clinic. "It's a tough routine. They don't baby you."

He was soon telling Mays and Snider about the letters he received while at the clinic—maybe twenty thousand in all, from friends and fans wishing him well.

"I couldn't believe some of them," he said. "They were incredibly kind, and a lot of them were from drunks who had gone through similar problems. Everybody wanted to congratulate me for stopping and everybody seemed to say the same thing—that Betty Ford was a lot tougher than Whitey Ford. A few guys could handle Whitey. Nobody could handle Betty."

It was nearing half past eight now, and the long program was just beginning. Smith moved through the introductions. Some players were booed. Others were simply ignored. Awards were handed out to many of the current stars. Small acceptance speeches were made. Baseball officials and former players in the audience were introduced to the crowd. Few members of the audience seemed to care. Their reaction made it clear that most in the audience were still angry with the striking players. They cared little about their attendance and wanted to get to the heart of the evening.

Soon the ballroom lights were dimmed. Composer and singer Terry Cashman was on stage. The band started playing. A film appeared on a huge screen. Cashman began singing his number, "Talkin' Baseball," which included the line, "Willie, Mickey and the Duke."

The audience applauded as their names were mentioned. Now segments from World Series films, pennant races, private photos, and team shots appeared on the screen. One photograph showed Snider and Mays together back in the early 1950s, certainly not as early as that lamented 1951 Brooklyn season. Then there was the first glimpse of Mantle standing at home plate. He was batting left-handed and the huge number seven on his uniform shirt could be seen in the picture. The crowd began to cheer. Many stood in the audience, and a spotlight on the dais caught Mantle with a shy grin.

"He leaned over to me when his picture came up on the screen the first time," Mays later said, "and he asked me, 'Were we ever that young?' I told him I was. I didn't know about him. He giggled."

In the darkened room, on that screen, the swing was perfect. The ball climbed high above the stadium, crashed into the stands in the third deck, and bounced back on the field.

Mantle could be seen jogging around first base, his head down, his elbows close to his sides, his eyes fixed on the dirt. As he came toward home plate, Yogi Berra, in that film and sitting nearby on the dais, grinned.

There were other shots of Mantle, hitting right-handed, running the bases, shaking hands after a home run, catching a ball with a brilliant effort. This one, hit by Gil Hodges of the Brooklyn Dodgers in the 1956 World Series, saved Don Larsen's perfect game.

It was too much for some people in the audience. They yelled Mickey's name and applauded him. He sat on the dais, looking straight at the screen, ignoring their chants, watching his younger self in a more satisfying time.

Films of Snider, Mays, and Mantle were all shown before the three were finally introduced as winners of the first annual Willie, Mickey and the Duke Award for Excellence.

Snider was called to talk first. He spoke of the joys of being back in New York, the loyalty of fans, and the thrill of being part of this special night.

"I'll come back any time you want me," he said.

Mays was next. He had been shy as a youngster, but had grown more secure in his maturity. The crowd hushed as he talked about the pleasures he had experienced playing in New York and the memories that stayed with him all his days.

"I'm just excited to be here tonight and to be part of this event," he said. "I know now that my name and the names of all three of us will last in this town with this award. Players will win this fifty—a hundred years from now, and they will ask about Duke Snider, Mickey Mantle and Willie Mays. People will tell them about us forever. I was part of this town and part of the history, and now I know that after I'm dead I will be remembered forever here. I just want to thank you all from the bottom of my heart."

He sat down to a huge roar of approval and shook hands with Snider and Mantle.

Now Claire Smith moved to introduce Mantle. He looked down at the dinner program in front of him. He seemed edgy as her introduction included a reference to his health problems. She finally, simply, said in a quiet voice, "Ladies and gentlemen, Mickey Mantle."

As it had for forty-five years, the name resonated through the room. He walked to the microphone amidst huge applause. He stood for a moment and looked out at the crowd. He shook his head, as if in disbelief that he was here, after months of health problems and his commitment to a new life style.

"They tell me I was here a few years ago and I don't even remember it," he said. "There are lots of things I don't remember."

The audience laughed at the self-deprecating humor, the folksy style, the Oklahoma twang that remained in his voice after all these years.

"I just want to thank the baseball writers for inviting me and I want to thank all you fans for showing up here tonight. I know it's been a tough baseball year and I hope they get all this labor stuff settled. I want the game to be what I remember it was," he said.

He mentioned what Mays had said about being remembered long after each of them was gone. He could have repeated his famous 1956 line at congressional hearings in Washington when Congress considered baseball's reserve clause. Casey Stengel had talked in convoluted sentences for forty-five minutes before Mantle was called by Senator Estes Kefauver for his opinions on the reserve clause.

"My view are just about the same as Casey's," said Mantle to a laughing congressional audience.

Now he chose his words carefully.

"I'm grateful for everything," he said. "I loved playing here, I loved the fans, and I think they appreciated me."

The dinner was over now, and Mantle returned to his restaurant on Central Park South. He talked with several friends for an hour or so and then retired to his apartment upstairs from the restaurant. He drank one soft drink.

The next day he would board a flight for his Dallas home.

Mickey Mantle was gone from New York. Forever.

It's 1951 and New York has yet to discover Mickey Mantle.

Phenom

New York City had three big-league baseball teams in 1951. The New York Giants played in the Polo Grounds on 155th Street and Eighth Avenue in Manhattan's Harlem, the Brooklyn Dodgers played in Ebbets Field on Bedford Avenue and Sullivan Place in Brooklyn, and the New York Yankees played in Yankee Stadium on 161st Street and River Avenue in the Bronx.

All three were in first place at the end of the regular season—the Dodgers and Giants tied for the National League pennant while the Yankees won their third pennant in a row in the American League.

About ten months before that glorious New York end to the baseball season, a sportswriter with the *New York Herald Tribune* named Harold Rosenthal put a letter into the mail to a Yankee prospect in Commerce, Oklahoma. A custom among many baseball writers in those simpler times, before agents, business managers, and lawyers surrounded a young ballplayer and dominated his deeds, was seeking out off-season stories. These were known in the trade as Hot Stove League stories because, supposedly, people in baseball's earliest years sat around a hot stove during the winter months and talked over the game.

"Arthur [Red] Patterson had come up with the brainchild of writing rookies each winter asking them about themselves. These rookie stories would give the fans something to talk about, get the clubs a little publicity and give the new player a little exposure," Rosenthal said.

Patterson had done this letter writing to rookies for several years as a sportswriter on the *Tribune*. By 1951 he was the press agent for the Yankees and encouraged Rosenthal to follow his lead.

"The clubs will give you the home addresses of the kids," Patterson told Rosenthal. "Just write them and ask them to tell you something about themselves, things like who their heroes are, what other sports they've played, anyone else in the family who are athletes, things like that. And by the way, write to this kid the Yankees had in Class B last season in Joplin. Name's Mantle and they think he's got a pretty good chance, although he's a shortstop and Phil Rizzuto was MVP last year."

Mantle, after two professional seasons in baseball at Independence, Kansas, where he batted .313 in 89 games, and at Joplin, Missouri, where he busted up the league with a .383 mark at the age of eighteen, was spending the winter near his Commerce home and working in the mines in nearby Picher, Oklahoma. He worked on motors. He carried cans around the mines. He drove a truck for supplies, shoveled zinc into carts, and did odd jobs.

Rosenthal sent out his letters to several players early in January of 1951. A few days later a letter came to the *Tribune* office in Manhattan. It was postmarked January 8, 1951, from Commerce, Oklahoma.

Mantle's name had appeared in the *Tribune* a couple of times before—when he signed in 1949 and, more importantly, when the Yankees listed him among the young players to be brought up at the end of the 1950 season. He had joined the Yankees September 17, 1950, in Sportsman's Park, St. Louis, just prior to a Yankee doubleheader with the St. Louis Browns.

Manager Casey Stengel told the sportswriters that day that Mantle was their prize youngster and had a big-league future. None of the sportswriters bothered to speak with the newcomer. They were too busy talking to the established stars and sizing the Yankees up for the 1950 World Series against the Philadelphia Phillies Whiz Kids.

In January of the next year, the Yankees announced they would invite some of their best young players to an early spring training camp in Phoenix, Arizona. They had switched sites with the Giants from St.

Petersburg, Florida, for that spring. The Yankees called it an instructional school. Stengel began defining it as a "structural" school.

Rosenthal's letter to Mantle resulted in a quick response. It was published the next day in its entirety in the *New York Herald Tribune*.

After the date January 8, 1951, written in printed, block letters on the top of a lined, white five-and-dime sheet of paper, the youngster had begun his letter with the greeting, "Mr. H. Rosenthal."

This was written by a boy of nineteen, who had graduated from high school a year and a half earlier, just after he had turned seventeen and a half. He had worked on his Commerce High newspaper because he knew so much about sports, but he had little interest in developing writing skills. Here was a youngster who from his earliest years was pointed in one direction only: to baseball.

I will answer your letter that I received the other day. You'll have to pardon the paper and pencil.

Tom Greenwade signed me from the Baxter Springs Ban Johnson team I was playing on. My background in baseball wasn't very much before I got into pro ball. I started playing in a Gabby Street league when I was 12 & played with Baxter 2 years and then signed with Independence when I got out of school at 17.

I don't have any relatives playing any sports. I guess until I was 17 I was a lot better fielder than hitter because I was never much bigger than a baseball bat. But last season I would say my hitting was better than my fielding as I led the league in errors with an even 50, but I also led in strikeouts so it's about a draw.

I have always played S.S. & Phil Rizzuto was always my idol.

I got my ankle kicked in football practice in '46 & it bruised the bone & that caused TB of the bone.

I'm not the only child as there are 3 more brothers and a sister in our family. Two of my brothers are twins & are going to be good athletes. I'm the oldest but they are about as big.

Well, I guess I've ans. all the questions for you. So I'll say good-bye for now."

The letter ended with a printed signature, "MICKEY MANTLE."

The original of the letter now resides in the Oklahoma Sports Hall of Fame where Rosenthal contributed it about ten years ago. "I wish I had retained it and sold it instead," Rosenthal said. I'd have been able to buy everyone a drink at the Baseball Writers Dinner in New York and thrown in a lavish tip."

A week or two later Mantle received another important letter from New York. This one was from Yankees farm director Lee MacPhail. He instructed Mantle to report to the Yankees early camp in Phoenix on February 15, 1951, about ten days before the rest of the big-league players were due to arrive.

Mantle had not received a train ticket for the journey from Commerce to the Yankees camp in Phoenix. He had not received any expense money to pay for meals or lodging when he got there, so he didn't respond.

MacPhail, concerned about his young charge, contacted the nearest newspaper, the *Miami Daily New Record.* They promised to send a reporter to Mantle's home in Commerce, which had no phone, and find out why Mantle had not made the trip to camp.

Ball clubs often forgot in those days—and maybe even today—that many youngsters at the beginning of their careers are not sophisticated in the ways of the world. Few would think of traveling to a training camp, a huge expense to those with limited finances, without a paid ticket and some spending money.

When the sportswriter from the local paper heard Mantle's story, he suggested Mickey call the Yankees office in New York. Mantle went to the administration office of the mine where he worked the next day, put in a collect call to the Yankees offices at 745 Fifth Avenue in Manhattan, and spoke to MacPhail.

"We'll get a ticket to you tomorrow," promised MacPhail, more than a little annoyed that the youngster they had such hopes for was wasting precious training days at home.

Tom Greenwade, the scout who had signed Mantle in 1949, arrived from his Kansas City home with a one-way train ticket to Phoenix and five ten-dollar bills for expenses.

Mickey Mantle was soon on his way to a big-league spring training camp.

If nothing more than going to spring training had ever happened in baseball for Mickey Mantle, it might have been enough for his father. Elvin "Mutt" Mantle had worked the mines around Commerce, spent time as a sharecropper, worked as a grader on highways, and played ball on weekends. He met and married Lovell Richardson, a neighborhood girl who was attracted to the tall, handsome, rugged-looking laborer.

On October 20, 1931, Mickey Charles Mantle, the young couple's first child, was born in a small, cluttered wooden home in Sapavinaw. The country was in the depths of the Great Depression.

Mutt Mantle thought only of making that youngster a big-league ballplayer.

Oklahoma was as hard hit as any state in the union by the depression. Farms were drought ridden, plagued by severe winds, and had a general lack of farm machinery. Many farmers who went broke abandoned their land, driving rickety cars west to California.

A little more than a year after Mickey Mantle was born, Franklin D. Roosevelt was elected President of the United States. He moved quickly after his inauguration to create what he called a New Deal—a chance for people to come out of the tragedy of this economic torture into a new and better life. Banks were closed, then reorganized. Businesses soon got small loans. The government was providing some financial aid, many new programs, and a great sense of optimism.

Oklahomans, like Mutt Mantle, were fiercely independent, strong-willed people. They benefited from the change of direction their government was taking.

Mickey's father never looked for a handout or a favor. He worked during all the desperate years of the depression. Mickey, his three younger brothers, and his sister all ate well, had a decent home, and attended school. They survived the struggle.

As tough a man as Mutt Mantle was, he'd met his match in his wife. Lovell Mantle was a fiercely proud woman. She asked no favors and got none. She cared for her brood, raised vegetables in her small garden, sewed clothes at home, and stretched out Mutt Mantle's meager earnings into adequate care for the family's needs.

Depression tales are replete with families like the Mantle family—surviving against incredible odds, pushing forward, asking for little, and accepting the will of God. What Mickey Mantle understood intuitively—what so many children of poor families understand—was that life is not fair. While some were wealthy, poverty was far more common. Youngsters from these bitterly poor backgrounds appreciated that they were in similar circumstances to their neighbors. That helped them to accept the grinding poverty. No one despises being poor when everyone else around them is experiencing the same hardships.

Mantle, in later years, would always be generous with money to friends and family. The extreme poverty of his youth, however, would often color his intensity when it was time to negotiate salary. His Yankee holdouts would be as bitter and emotional as those experienced by any player on any team in baseball history.

On a chilly February morning in 1951, both of his parents drove him to the railroad station in Vinita, Oklahoma, some fifty miles from Commerce, which was the nearest railroad junction for the area. Mickey Mantle began his long journey to Yankee stardom with a railroad trip to Phoenix.

He had filled a straw suitcase with a couple of pairs of Levi dungarees, two shirts, socks, underwear, a sports jacket for dining in the hotel, one tie, and his Marty Marion baseball glove, an endorsed model named after the famed St. Louis Cardinals shortstop, his favorite player on his favorite team for most of his early years.

There hadn't been much conversation in that car, Mickey later reported. His parents were not talkers. The excitement of setting out for spring training was too great. They all realized that things in the Mantle household would never again be quite the same.

Spring training is the most joyous time of the year for veteran players, and the most terrifying for youngsters.

The older players, certain of their jobs, coast through the early morning workouts, kid with each other, banter about the girls in the stands, criticize the club management and the press, and await the daily arrival of old pals from other clubs, once the games begin.

For youngsters, especially one as young and naive as Mantle, it can be fraught with terror. All the other players seem to know each other. All the other players are familiar with the routine, the time it takes to dress, the early exercises, the intense workouts, the small lunches of soup, carrots, and juice, and the scheduling of golf dates and early evening dinners.

For a youngster such as Mantle, all of this raised apprehension and fear. Don't make noise in the clubhouse. Don't call attention to yourself. Don't violate any rules—known or unknown.

The first morning, Mantle shared a cab to the ballpark from the team hotel with two other rookies, Tom Morgan and Andy Carey. He arrived at the clubhouse to find several of the players from the 1950 season already in camp for some early work.

It was not unusual for veteran players to show up early at a spring training camp if they had signed their contracts. Most of them lived in cold climates. Most of them held boring winter jobs. All of them craved the sun, the excitement, and the fraternalism of a baseball camp.

On that first day, one player, Billy Martin, a backup infielder who had played all of 34 games in his rookie season, quickly came over to young Mantle. Martin had a big nose, a bony face with dark eyes, and a squeaky voice.

"Hi ya, pardner," he said to the young Oklahoman.

"Mantle," Mickey replied.

"Yeah, yeah, we all know who you are. We read the sports pages," Martin said.

The early spring camp, Casey's "structural" school, had gotten a lot of press because it had not been tried before. Teams never spent extra money for an early training camp for rookies. If a club had a promising rookie, they would bring him in when the regulars reported. The Yankees had so many promising rookies that year—Mantle, Andy Carey, Tom Morgan, Gil McDougald, Moose Skowron, Tom Sturdivant, and a dozen more—that they decided to bring them all in together for a concentrated look.

Martin had played only one big-league season, but his pugnacious personality and his big mouth had gained him a great deal of attention.

He had grown up in a blue-collar neighborhood in Berkeley, California. His father had abandoned him, and he had been raised by his feisty mother and grandfather and, later on, by a stepfather. Martin had played ball on the city streets, in city parks, and on a few amateur teams before signing with the minor-league Oakland club in 1946. The manager of that team was Casey Stengel. Martin became a surrogate son to the childless Stengel.

When Stengel was brought to New York in 1949 from Oakland, his reputation preceded him. Stengel had been a colorful character as a player in Brooklyn and with the New York Giants. He was an even wilder personality as a manager in Brooklyn and with the Brooklyn National League team.

After Stengel had been fired numerous times during his baseball career, Oakland had appeared to be his last job—until he had great success there.

The Yankees had fired Bucky Harris after the 1948 season. General manager George Weiss, who had worked with Stengel in the minor leagues in the 1920s, recommended hiring Stengel to Yankee owners Dan Topping and Del Webb.

Lee MacPhail, the farm director and son of flamboyant Larry MacPhail, who had run the Brooklyn team, knew Stengel's reputation. "My God," he told his staff, "we've hired a clown."

The "clown" won a pennant and World Series with the Yankees in 1949 and repeated in 1950. Now he was attempting his third championship in a row. Martin expected to contribute.

"Mickey looked lost those first days," said Martin. "He was just a scared kid and I'd been around. I just took him under my wing."

How a backup infielder, only twenty-two years old himself that spring, expected to lead a 19-year-old, only Billy seemed to know.

"Billy had an air of confidence no other young player I knew ever had," recalled Whitey Ford.

Martin, Mantle, and later Ford, who joined the team late in 1950 and did not arrive in a Yankee camp again until he'd finished his two years of military service in 1953, became the closest of baseball friends. They would remain so until Martin's death in an automobile accident on Christmas Day of 1989, near Martin's farm in Johnson City, New York.

"I remember when I first came to the club in the spring of 1950," Martin said. "I walked into the clubhouse and there was the great Joe DiMaggio. He was an awesome figure around that team. People would clear a path for him when he walked to his locker and nobody would say hello unless he said hello to them first. He was like a senator, a king, some divine royalty. I just yelled over, 'Hey, dago,' and he laughed. We were good friends from that day on. He always wanted to eat dinner with me—in the hotel room if we lost and in a fancy restaurant where he picked up the tab if we won. Boy, did I root for us to win."

In the early days of batting practice that spring, Mantle was already drawing notice from his teammates. The baseballs were rocketing off his bat from both sides of the plate. Huge drives would crash against the stands or fly completely out of the small minor-league park and into the light air at Phoenix.

"I remember when I first saw him," said Ralph Houk, a backup catcher in those days and later a Yankee manager. "It was something none of us had ever seen. He just hit the ball so hard it was unreal. Each shot seemed to be harder and farther than the one before. He was hitting the rookie pitchers early, of course, and the regular pitchers when they came in and then the opposing pitchers when we started playing games.

"It got so that the most exciting event of the day was Mickey in batting practice," said Houk. "No matter what else was going on—running drills, sliding, fielding, conditioning—it would all stop when Mickey walked into the cage to bat left-handed or right-handed. There was never anything like it."

Mantle worked out with the other infielders and studied the moves of Phil Rizzuto, the longtime Yankees shortstop who was coming off a most valuable player year. It did him little good. He was awkward in the field, couldn't make a double play smoothly, and threw the ball wildly from shortstop most of the time.

Stengel knew he had a gem of a hitter who should not be bothered with the intricacies of fielding the shortstop position. Harry Craft, who had managed Mantle in the minor leagues, suggested the kid should play the outfield.

Stengel sent Mantle out with the outfielders the next day. Tommy Henrich, a marvelous Yankee outfielder who had retired after the 1950 season, worked with the young outfielders. He gave Mantle special attention.

"You could see that incredible ability," said Henrich. "He could run like the wind, he had a very strong arm and he had those marvelous base-ball instincts. Much of that is God given. I believe that. You can only teach some of the game—the subtlety, the finesse, the positioning. You can't teach the physical things. Mantle just had it when he showed up. You'd have to be a fool not to recognize that."

Henrich, nicknamed "Old Reliable" by the New York press for his skills as a hitter in the clutch, showered knowledge on the youngster. He hit dozens and dozens of fly balls to him, this way and that, in and out, hard bouncers in front of him and line drives over his head. Henrich was as stylish with the bat as any man around the game. The variety of prac-tice balls with Henrich paid off for Mantle.

Exhibition games began early—against the Cleveland Indians who trained nearby and other big-league clubs who traveled to Phoenix. They also played college and amateur teams.

"He just started hitting home runs—it seemed like every day," said Houk. "Some of them would just take your breath away. We knew we had something special here."

"He's got it in his body to be one of the greatest," said Stengel, who seemed awed by the youngster. Stengel had played against Babe Ruth, Ty Cobb, and Rogers Hornsby. None of them, he said, had overwhelmed him like this kid when he stood at home plate.

The sportswriters began writing glowing stories about Mantle for the readers back home. Shortly after the games began, local papers print-ed the New York exhibition schedule. Fans wanted to know when the Yankees and Brooklyn Dodgers would meet in three spring games at the Stadium and at Ebbets Field before the 1951 opener.

DiMaggio had announced early that spring that he intended to retire after the 1951 season. His body was wearing down. Joe's brother, Tom, ran the family restaurant at Fisherman's Wharf in San Francisco. He was asked years later why Joe had retired after the 1951 season at the age of thirty-six. The Yankees had offered him a contract for two more years at the princely 1951 sum of $100,000 per year.

"Don't you know? He wasn't Joe DiMaggio anymore," said Tom DiMaggio.

There was a standard of excellence that DiMaggio had set for him-self. He recognized that he could no longer achieve it. He chose to retire rather than tarnish his reputation, his name, and his romantic stature in baseball lore.

Mantle's outstanding success dovetailed that spring with DiMaggio's intended retirement.

Even before DiMaggio was gone from the Yankees scene, sportswriters had anointed his successor. Mickey Mantle would take over Joe's position in center field and Joe's standing with the team.

The Yankees marched through the spring games with ease. Mantle seemed to homer every other day. When he didn't hit a home run, he struck out. His strikeouts would be almost an equal thrill for observers as he drove the bat around his body, followed through in a whipping motion, and almost fell to his knees. He kicked up much home plate dust.

His swings from each side of the plate were quite different. From the right side, his natural side, he appeared to hit the top of the ball, driving line drive home runs over the fence by a few feet, the ball crashing against a wall with a huge thud. The home runs from the left side of the plate would get the bottom of the baseball, loft it into the air in a huge arch, and then fall gracefully against a distant seat.

Either way, it was a show that few observers of baseball had ever seen.

Mantle put on a stirring show at an exhibition in Los Angeles at the University of Southern California campus. He hit two huge home runs, a triple, and a single. Rod Dedeaux, the USC coach, who had played a couple of games in Brooklyn when Stengel was managing there, was a close friend of the Yankee manager.

"I asked Casey if he would bring the team out for an exhibition against our college kids," said Dedeaux. "It was a thrilling event for us. When Mantle put on that show, he almost broke down a couple of our buildings. There was never anyone quite like Mickey."

It was almost time to go east. The Yankees were to play an exhibition at the home park of their Kansas City farm club before traveling by train to New York where they would meet the Dodgers in three weekend games.

Mantle had received a letter earlier from his draft board in Commerce that he had to be examined for military service. Many young men, including several teammates, were serving military time during the heightened draft period of the Korean War. Mantle, because of his osteomyelitis, had earlier been rejected by the draft board and placed in the 4F category.

Now some nasty letters were being printed in newspapers. There were those who thought the 19-year-old should not be playing baseball while other 19-year-olds were dying in the Korean War.

Mantle went back home, took the exam again, and, once again declared physically unfit, rejoined the Yankees in New York.

Before the first exhibition game in Brooklyn, Stengel marched his young outfielder out to the right field wall at Ebbets Field for a little indoctrination about that tricky fence. The wall in Ebbets Field, hard against Bedford Avenue, had a screen on top where home runs were turned into doubles. It combined wood and concrete together, and the combination forced batted balls every which way.

Stengel had a bag of balls and threw them at the wall, dancing this way and that in getting them on one bounce. Typical of Stengel, he related much of his Brooklyn career while Mantle stared at the tricky fence. This was something he had never seen back in Oklahoma, in the two previous pro leagues he had played in, or anywhere else he had played baseball.

Mantle's eyes seemed to glaze over as Stengel's rapid-fire stream of consciousness stirred feelings of doubt. Could he really play here? Could he play that wall without embarrassing himself in front of his famous teammates and the New York fans?

"I played here. You can learn to play that wall if you watch," said Stengel.

"You mean you actually played here?" asked an astonished Mantle.

"For crissakes, you think I was born old?" said Stengel.

Mantle never had difficulty in the game in right field, so the lesson proved academic. By the time Mantle returned to Ebbets Field to play against the Dodgers in 1953, he was the team's center fielder. Right field would be Hank Bauer's problem.

Mantle hit his 14th home run of the spring that day in his 34th game of spring training. He had a double and two singles, caught everything hit to him, and finished the exhibition season with a .402 average.

Nothing had officially been said to Mantle about becoming a member of the New York Yankees for 1951. There had been no mention of a major-league contract.

Traveling secretary Frank Scott posted a sign in the clubhouse about travel plans to Washington, where the season was supposed to begin for the Yankees against the Washington Senators.

Mantle watched DiMaggio dress for the trip. He wore a dark suit with wide lapels, a blue tie, a starched white shirt, and gleaming shoes, made so by the endless polishing of the clubhouse man. DiMaggio tipped extra for a glowing getaway day shine.

Mantle put on his one sports jacket and tie. He followed Billy Martin to the bus outside of Ebbets Field, which would take the team to Grand Central Station for the journey south to Washington, DC.

Mantle sat with Billy Martin. Yogi Berra sprawled across the seat with a comic book. Hank Bauer, Gene Woodling, Joe Collins, Allie Reynolds, Vic Raschi, and Ralph Houk were engaged in a card game. Phil Rizzuto immediately went to sleep.

Stengel sat in the drawing room of the private car with general manager George Weiss and several of his coaches—Jim Turner, Frank Crosetti, and Bill Dickey.

Weiss and Stengel decided it was time to put the young Mantle under contract. They looked down the car to where Mantle and Martin were thumbing through a few magazines. Crosetti was dispatched to bring Mantle back to the drawing room, which included a small desk and lamp.

Weiss said, "Mickey, we want you on the Yankees. You have to sign this contract."

"Yes, sir," said Mantle.

Weiss pulled a fountain pen from his inside coat pocket. He had a contract on the small desk opened to the final page. He showed Mantle where to sign, and without another word, Mantle signed his first Yankee contract for $5000 a year.

The contract, with the reserve clause in force at the time, bound Mantle to the Yankees for life unless sold, traded, or released, a clause players would later overturn in establishing free agency.

Mantle would never make over $100,000 a season, while several players in baseball cleared the seven million dollar year mark in the mid-nineties.

The Yankees arrived in Washington, DC, and took several waiting cabs to the Shoreham Hotel, a huge Washington landmark with one of the largest outdoor pools of any hotel in America.

Mantle and Martin went to the hotel coffee shop upon arrival for a sandwich. They drank a couple of beers and settled into their room for the night. The baseball season would open the next afternoon in Washington. President Harry Truman was expected to attend and throw out the first ball, a tradition that had existed ever since President William Howard Taft established the custom in 1912.

Early spring rains drenched the East Coast that April, and the Yankees never got to play the opener in Washington. They journeyed back to New York after three days.

Mantle stayed at the Grand Concourse Hotel in the Bronx, a short walk to Yankee Stadium. He arrived before any of the other players. His baggy uniform, with the large number seven on its back, was hung neatly in his locker.

Clubhouse man Pete Sheehy had been doing this kind of thing since 1926. He placed Mantle in a far corner of the locker room, where the

Yankee rookies traditionally gathered. Opposite Mantle was the locker of Yogi Berra, and all the way down, near the trainer's room, was DiMaggio's locker.

"That was so Joe wouldn't get tired walking into the trainer's room before a game," said Martin.

Mantle hardly cared where his locker was located. He was now, finally, in the most famous sports arena in all America, "the House that Ruth Built," the famed Yankee Stadium.

Sheehy, wise in these ways, fully understood that young Mantle was heading for stardom. He had given him that low number seven because he believed the number three of Babe Ruth, the number four of Lou Gehrig, and the number five of Joe DiMaggio was about to be joined in Yankee lore by another single-digit uniformed star.

Mantle was on Stengel's lineup card for right field that first game. Jackie Jensen was leading off in left field, Phil Rizzuto was batting second at shortstop, Mantle batted third, DiMaggio batted fourth, Yogi batted fifth, Johnny Mize, who had been acquired mostly for pinch hitting, was sixth. Gil McDougald was at third, Jerry Coleman was at second, and Vic Raschi was the starter against the Boston Red Sox.

Mantle grounded out twice and then singled off left-hander Bill Wight.

In those conservative baseball days, nothing was made of a youngster's first big-league hit. Mantle's heart may have been pounding a little faster. He may have been laughing inside with the joy of it. His body may have tingled all over. Nobody made a fuss in that pretelevision era.

Getting a base hit in a big-league game was no event. It was expected, especially if the player doing it was wearing a Yankee uniform and had crushed so many baseballs that spring in Arizona.

The Yankees were in Chicago on May 1, 1951. Randy Gumbert, a hard-throwing right-hander, was the starter for the White Sox. He threw Mantle a high, inside fastball. The youngster got around on it and drove it deep into the stands at the old ballpark. Fans scurried for the ball as Mantle ran rapidly around the bases.

There was little fuss on the field when a Yankee homered. They were the Bronx Bombers, weren't they?

That home run ball would disappear into the stands, into the hands of some scurrying youngster, as Mantle came around to be congratulated by DiMaggio with a mild handshake at the plate and a few other warm responses in the dugout.

Five hundred and thirty-five more homers would follow.

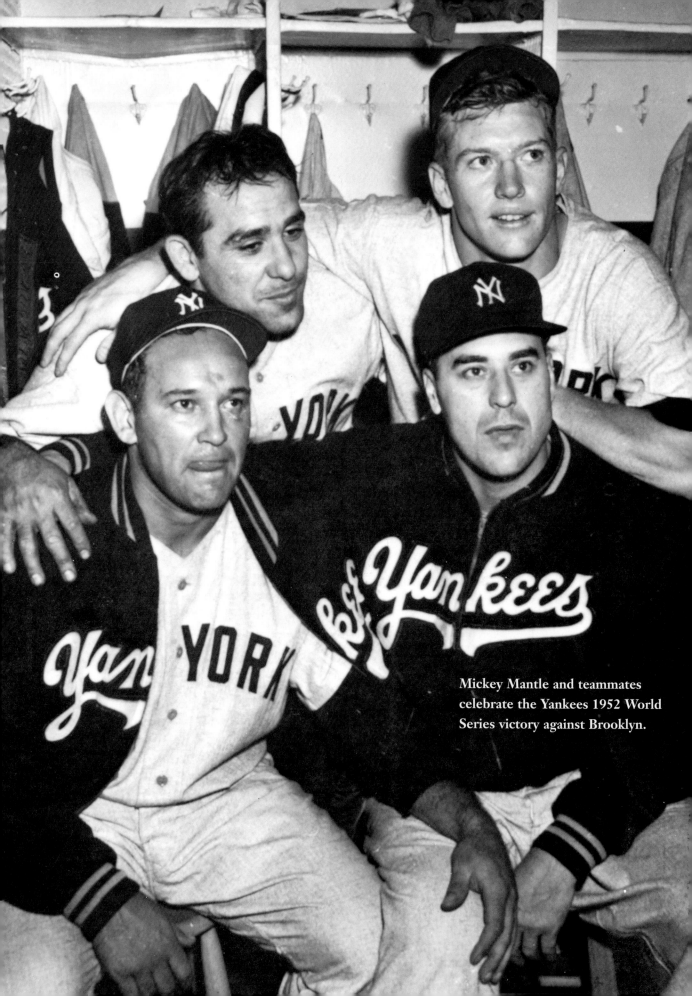

Mickey Mantle and teammates celebrate the Yankees 1952 World Series victory against Brooklyn.

Three

The Heir Apparent

There is a rhythm to a baseball team's history, especially a team as glamorous as the New York Yankees.

Old stars leave and new ones arrive. Careers in baseball are finite. Each day in the game is one day less for a player, one day closer to the end.

There is always tension around an aging player when he sees the end clearly in sight. Sportswriter Frankie Graham of the *New York Journal American* wrote of a crusty Yankees outfielder, Bob Meusel, in the late 1920s, "He learned to say hello when it was time to say good-bye."

Babe Ruth joined the Yankees in 1920 and left in anger in 1934. Lou Gehrig joined the Yankees in 1923 and left in sadness in 1939.

Ruth, baseball's home run king, batted only .288 with 22 home runs in his final season as a Yankee in 1934. Gehrig had a Triple Crown season that year with a league-leading .363 average, 49 home runs, and 165 RBI.

In 1936 Gehrig batted .354 and led the league in home runs with 49, but the attention that year focused on a youngster from San Francisco named Joseph Paul DiMaggio Jr.

DiMaggio batted .323 as a rookie in 1936 with 29 home runs. Gehrig ended his consecutive-game steak in Detroit on May 2, 1939, with 2,130 consecutive games played.

DiMaggio led the league with a .381 average in Gehrig's final 1939 year.

By then the Yankees were DiMaggio's team. He was the player opposing teams concentrated on. A brilliant hitter and a magnificent fielder, he ran bases without mistakes and could throw hard and accurately. He struck out only 369 times in thirteen seasons, a remarkable record for a slugger who hit 361 home runs. He batted in 56 consecutive games in 1941, a streak that had the entire country on edge.

"Did Joe get a hit today?" was a question heard often on the streets of New York, on California's ocean beaches, in the cotton fields of the South, the windswept plains of the Midwest, and in fishing villages across New England. It was an exciting summer.

A song entitled "Joltin' Joe DiMaggio" was written by Alan Courtney and Ben Homer and introduced by Les Brown and his orchestra in the middle of the streak.

> *He'll live in Baseball's Hall of Fame.*
> *He got there blow by blow.*
> *Our kids will tell their kids his name,*
> *Joltin' Joe DiMaggio.*

Joltin' Joe DiMaggio. The Yankee Clipper. The Big Guy. Those were the names the newspapers called him. "The Dago" was a term used endearingly by some close friends and teammates about the Italian hero from San Francisco in a less politically correct time.

The streak had made DiMaggio a national figure. One need not know or care about baseball to recognize his name. He was as famous and popular a man as there was in America in his playing days.

In the summer of 1941, while the streak was growing, he attended the Joe Louis–Billy Conn heavyweight championship fight in Yankee Stadium. He walked down the aisle to his seat with famed New York restaurateur Toots Shor and famed novelist Ernest Hemingway. Fans shouted his name, "Joe, Joe, Joe," as he marched stoically ahead. A youngster spotted the bearded man walking with him.

"Hey," the kid asked Hemingway, "are you anybody?"

"Yeah," replied Hemingway as he pointed to DiMaggio, "I'm his doctor."

DiMaggio left for military service in 1943 and did not return until 1946. He had four more marvelous seasons in the next five years.

By 1951, his final season, he was thirty-six years old. He was suffering from a chronic bad heel. His shoulder ached. He was under a doctor's care for his ulcers.

DiMaggio had always been aloof from most of his teammates. Eddie

Lopat, a left-handed pitcher who spent four seasons as a teammate, said he was the loneliest man he had ever seen.

"When we are on the road," said Lopat, "he leads the league in room service."

DiMaggio lived alone in a New York hotel apartment. In the off-season he lived in a big house in San Francisco with his sister. He seemed to have a coterie of hangers-on. Few could be identified as friends.

Teammates rarely spoke to him. Members of the press were careful around him. Even manager Casey Stengel paid homage to him.

Stengel was working on his lineup one day as reporters badgered him for the names. Stengel verbally danced around the subject for a few minutes. The reporters pressed harder.

DiMaggio, tying his shoe laces a few feet away, had been ailing. He looked over toward Stengel and caught his eye. DiMaggio nodded slightly.

"Now I can give you the lineup," Stengel shouted, recognizing that DiMaggio had decided to play that day.

In the spring of 1951, DiMaggio made clear to reporters that he was almost certain about retirement at the end of the season.

There should have been massive attention on him as he played his final Yankee games, but that was the spring Mickey Mantle exploded on the Yankee scene.

"Joe was hurting and getting ready at his own pace, the way he always did," said Phil Rizzuto. "Mantle just came in and hit those huge home runs and everybody hounded him."

The 19-year-old Mantle was in awe of DiMaggio. DiMaggio, 36 years old, was envious of Mantle.

Every Mantle home run only reminded DiMaggio of his mortality. Every Mantle story in the press only forced home the traditional recognition of the team torch being passed.

"I never even talked to him," Mantle said years later. "I was afraid to talk to him. He always seemed so distant. I was afraid of being rebuffed. Maybe it would have been different if I had asked for help. I just didn't know how."

DiMaggio that summer was struggling with his age. Mantle that summer was struggling with his youth.

DiMaggio labored through 116 games, batted .263, hit only 12 home runs, and announced his retirement in November.

Mantle hit .267 in 96 games, spent some six weeks in the Yankees Triple A farm team in Kansas City, and returning with renewed confidence, learned right field well in the Stadium and made it clear that he was ready to make the Yankees his team—while DiMaggio roamed in center field.

Stengel had trouble nursing DiMaggio through that summer. He respected Joe's ability and career impact. At the same time, he saw DiMaggio's skills diminishing. He had even tried to save DiMaggio some wear and tear by moving him to first base for a game the year before. DiMaggio, as proud as he was vain, saw that as a terrible affront to his standing as the game's most stylish center fielder.

Ralph Houk, the Yankees manager in 1967, moved Mantle to first base. In contrast to DiMaggio, Mantle willingly accepted the change, knowing full well his running speed was gone and that his shoulder no longer could handle the stress of tough throws. The calculated move meant his career might be lengthened.

Mantle would play first base modestly well in the final two seasons of his career in 1967 and 1968.

In 1951 reporters, always looking for new stars and new stories, spent more time and more space writing about the young Mantle coming in than they did about the old DiMaggio going out.

Few of the sportswriters, except perhaps Red Smith of the *Herald Tribune* and John Drebinger of the *New York Times*, had been around the Yankees when DiMaggio broke in that spring of 1936. These veteran scribes were outnumbered by younger reporters who could more easily relate to Mantle. Mickey was quiet and shy. DiMaggio was aloof. Mickey was boyish and charming. DiMaggio was standoffish and cold. Mickey was excited at every success. DiMaggio was laconic at every failure.

Unfortunately, Mantle was thrown into the eye of this storm. There were separate camps, as it were, among the press and the players in this subtle rivalry. Some reporters saw DiMaggio going out and moaned about it. Others accepted the reality of it and covered the young Mantle enthusiastically.

Reporters around a baseball team tend to write the stories they believe will gain the most attention for them. They struggle for bylines as young journalists; they struggle even harder for big stories and front-page stories as they grow older.

DiMaggio had been written about for fifteen years by then. There had been songs about him, dozens of magazine articles, many books, and even a film treatment of his life. He had been married to an actress named Dorothy Arnold and was later married to another actress named Marilyn Monroe. He had become a standard of excellence in the game.

By 1951 he was a tired story.

A scene that would repeat itself five more times while Mantle was a Yankee, a World Series victory for Yogi Berra and Mickey.

Ahh, Mantle. That was something else. Youthful, handsome, incredibly strong, properly shy and modest, eager, and so very new.

Neither could control the way the press played them that spring of 1951. Both felt the impact. DiMaggio became more withdrawn. Mantle became more exuberant.

It may be difficult in an examination of those times to fully appreciate the significance of baseball and its heroes in the early 1950s.

World War II had ended in 1945. Baseball was at its lowest ebb then. The 1946 season was a struggle to regain momentum. The 1947 season, with the coming of Jackie Robinson, put baseball once again on the front pages of many newspapers.

While many Americans might be interested in politics, theater, art, music, literature, history, economics, or architecture, almost all Americans were interested in baseball.

Television was a major factor by the spring of 1951. The World Series had been televised every year since 1947, and DiMaggio starred in three of the previous four Series events.

Professional football had not yet reached its maturity in 1951. Professional basketball had bounced around small gymnasiums for thirty or forty years and was still being played in such places as the Sixty-Ninth Regiment Armory in New York City by teams with names like the Fort Wayne Zollner Pistons.

Baseball was king. It was the sport most watched and most admired by young people. It was the most commercial in every aspect.

These were quiet times with few distractions. The economy was strong. The dream of owning homes, for most Americans, and especially for the World War II veterans, was being realized. There were cars in almost every garage—two in many. Grocery stores were filled with fresh, wholesome food. Employment was up, and the recreational dollar was plentiful.

While a war in Korea impacted this bucolic picture and a young Mantle would face off with his draft board, the universal trauma of World War II was gone. There was adequate time to examine baseball and baseball heroes at one's leisure.

Baseball had a grip on Americans that made many of its stars, probably starting with Babe Ruth, as important as any person in American life.

In 1930 when Ruth was asked if he was embarrassed that he made a larger salary, $80,000, than President Herbert Hoover did at $75,000, he replied, "I had a better year than he did."

No one resented the remark. The Babe was beloved. Hoover was a politician who by then, in the depths of the Great Depression, may have been as disliked as any man in the United States.

Mantle emerged in 1951 into an arena of public acceptance, joy, appreciation, and star watching, as DiMaggio was preparing to forsake his place.

There were several factors adding to the equation.

Mantle was joining the most famous team in sports, the team of Ruth, Gehrig, DiMaggio—the team that had dominated the game for so long and who in 1927 represented the best ever, the team that played in the most famous sports stadium in the country.

As television became more important in sports, DiMaggio—aging, grouchy, unsmiling—was on his way out.

Mantle—youthful, strikingly handsome with his blue eyes and

blonde hair, powerful, a little innocent and naive—was being seen in millions of homes.

If there is one single factor that contributed to Mantle's fame, stardom, and the loyalty of so many fans, it had to be his frequent appearances on television.

DiMaggio would always be admired, respected, and revered.

Mantle would always be loved, cherished, and fawned over.

When a young player takes the field as Mantle did for the first time against Boston at Yankee Stadium in 1951, he carries more than his bat with him.

"Seventy-five percent of the game is ninety-five percent in your head," Yogi Berra once said.

Berra may not have a strong sense of mathematics, but he had a genius for common sense. He understood that the batter, especially, takes his psyche to the plate each time. Is the pitcher better than I? Is he too smart for me? Will I embarrass myself? Do I really belong here? Is this all a mistake?

"Fear," sportswriter Leonard Koppett wrote in a book examining the essence of hitting. Hitting was all about the conquest of that fear—fear that the ball would strike you in the skull and kill you. (Only Ray Chapman, in 1920, ever died from a thrown ball off underhand pitcher Carl Mays.) There is fear that the reflexes will not work fast enough, fear that the split second necessary to make a decision about fastball against curveball, change-up against slider, high against low, inside against outside will not be nearly enough.

While DiMaggio's reflexes were losing reaction time that spring, Mantle's were growing quicker. He was doing much with the bat—a learned response from all the years in the Oklahoma ball fields, in the amateur leagues, in the two professional seasons he'd had, and from that incredible confidence he had gained after destroying big-league pitching all spring.

Berra also said, "You can't think and hit at the same time."

The greatest skill in sports is hitting a baseball thrown at incredible speeds. It was evident early on that Mantle had that dazzling skill. He had it from the right side of the plate and from the left side of the plate. He had bat speed, splendid reflexes, and superhuman power to drive a baseball huge distances. He needn't spend much time at the plate thinking.

Since, in Yogi's terms, so much of the game was in his head, his fierce determination to succeed cost him dearly in those early days. He would get his hits and blast an occasional homer. But more often he would be fooled by veteran pitchers and embarrassed at the plate. Too often he struck out. He struck out 1,710 times in his career and walked 1,734 times—figures he combined for a running gag.

"I played eighteen years in the big leagues, but I walked and struck out so much that I figure I only touched the ball about ten years of that time," he often said.

He swung the bat as ferociously as any man who ever played the game. He hit some of the most distant home runs. He also spun around after a miss at the plate more than any player.

Many times when he struck out, even in those earliest days, he would drag himself back to the dugout, hurl his batting helmet down the first baseline, pound the bat against the dugout wall as he went down the steps, attack a water cooler, and sit down on the bench with a huge thud.

"If you keep breaking up those bats and hats," Stengel once told him, "I'm gonna charge you for the equipment."

There were four hundred major-league players in baseball in those days of eight-team leagues. The competition for jobs was fierce, and the level of intensity at which the game was played was severe.

Mantle played hard most of the time, incredibly hard. But like many young players, especially when the strikeouts began piling up, he could be careless. His mind would wander, and he might miss a fly ball in right field, miss a sign from the manager at the plate, or pull off a bonehead play. When he was slumping, he liked to break an "oh-fer" day (no hits) with a drag bunt. He often picked the wrong time, especially in a close one-run game where a home run would tie it or win it for the Yankees.

On one occasion he ended a game with a drag bunt against St. Louis Browns pitcher Satchel Paige. It went foul with two strikes for strike three. Paige showed his appreciation with the tip of his cap.

Stengel showed his anger by yelling into the youngster's face, "If I want you to bunt, I'll tell you to bunt."

Mantle stopped doing that for a while but soon resorted to that favorite play of his, the drag bunt from the left side, for a base hit. It helped him break out of many a slump in his career.

By early July, with his average sinking, Stengel began considering a demotion to the minor leagues. It was clear that the pressure of playing for the Yankees, the constant comparisons with DiMaggio's rookie year, the references to his role as the Yankees' successor to the great ones like Ruth, Gehrig, and DiMaggio, and the expectations he had for his own accomplishments all began wearing Mantle down. With a mixed sense of frustration and recognition, Stengel decided to send him to the Yankees farm team at Kansas City.

Timing is vital in baseball, as it is in life. A little earlier and it could have been emotionally damaging to Mantle. A little later could have resulted in the same shattering of confidence. Many young players have brilliant springs, slow starts, and fast ends to their careers.

The Yankees were certain Mantle would not be one of those disappointing players. The talent was too obvious. However, it was time to move him away from New York, with its media attention, the nightlife of the city, the gawking girls outside the stadium, and all the attention his arrival had caused even before he had played a full season.

Mickey Mantle was on his way to the minors and a major turning point in his life and career.

Stengel had decided that Mantle at the age of nineteen simply was not up to the pressures. He knew the youngster needed some breathing room, a cooling-off period, an escape from the torment of failure.

As gently as possible, which was hardly his style, Stengel told Mantle he was being sent down to the Yankees farm club at Kansas City. He would join the Blues in Minneapolis.

The manager of Blues was George Selkirk. The Yankees could not have made a better choice for Mantle.

Selkirk was Canadian born, a tall, handsome man with wavy black hair and a commanding presence. The 43-year-old former Yankees outfielder had spent nine years with the team and played in six World Series. He had an impressive lifetime .290 average and a couple of World Series homers in 1936.

He understood better than almost anyone what Mantle was going through. Selkirk had been the man who succeeded Babe Ruth in right field for the Yankees.

"I was scared stiff when I first joined the club in '34," he once said. "I never knew when Babe would decide to take off a few innings or take off the game. Usually when I came out the fans would boo me, because I wasn't the Babe. All I could do was try my best."

In 1935 Ruth moved on to the Boston National League club for an ill-fated finish to his career, and Selkirk became the full-time right fielder. The pressure was enormous.

"The newspapermen kept asking what it felt like succeeding the Babe," he recalled. "I just told them I wasn't succeeding or replacing the Babe. Nobody could replace the Babe. I was just trying to establish myself as a big league ball player."

When Mantle, depressed, wary from the trip, anxious and unsure about the future, joined Selkirk's Kansas City club, the manager spent several minutes with him before the next game.

"I told Mickey he was just to relax and play ball like he always had.

He was here to regain his batting eye and his confidence. He just stared off into space," Selkirk said.

Knowing he was in a bad batting slump, Mantle chose to drag a bunt his first time at bat with Kansas City. It was not what Selkirk wanted. He chewed the youngster out and reminded him the Yankees wanted to see his batting eye and his power, not his running speed.

Mantle seemed lost with that Kansas City team made up mostly of over-the-hill players and poor prospects. He was not yet twenty years old and didn't easily join in clubhouse comedy. He was wound too tight with his own inner turmoil.

When the Blues returned to Kansas City, Mantle called his father at his job. Mantle told his father he couldn't hit big-league pitching, he couldn't hit Triple A pitching, and he was thinking of quitting. His father decided he would drive the five hours from Commerce, Oklahoma, in the northeast tip of the state, down to Kansas City to see his struggling son.

One can only imagine the thoughts racing through the head of the determined and hardheaded miner as he drove down those open roads in July of 1951. He had spent a good part of the past twenty years pushing his firstborn son into a life of baseball. He had strongly identified with Mickey's success. He himself had dreamed these same dreams. Circumstances had prevented him from reaching his goal, but it did not diminish his love for the game and the thrill he experienced as he saw his son maturing into a fine player. He had great hopes for Mickey's future.

If so much of the game, as Yogi Berra pointed out, was in Mickey's head, his self-esteem was at its lowest point when his father walked into the Aladdin Hotel.

Mickey greeted him shyly. His father exploded. He threw some of Mickey's clothes into a suitcase and reminded him that only a life of drudgery in the depths of the mines awaited him if he quit now.

"I thought I raised a man, not a coward," said Mutt Mantle to his dejected son.

Mickey backed away from his father. He accepted the reprimand as best he could. He promised that he would stay with baseball and would try even harder. Mutt Mantle shook his son's hand.

They soon parted. Mutt Mantle headed back to his job at the mines. Mickey Mantle headed back to his job on the ball field.

The visit, combined with the tough talk from his father, worked wonders. In a little more than a month at Kansas City, Mantle batted .361, hit 11 home runs in 40 games, knocked in an incredible 50 runs, walked 23 times, and struck out only 30 times.

"He just seemed to be more spirited, more in command of himself

Mantle would tower over the Brooklyn Dodgers in the 1952 World Series.

after his dad visited him," said Selkirk. "It was a great thing to see that change."

The Yankees, aware that Mantle had returned to his spring training form, brought him back to New York. They wanted to reward him for his efforts at Kansas City and prepare him for the World Series.

Mantle finished the regular season with a .267 average (modestly successful for a rookie), hit 13 home runs in 96 games, drove in 65 runs, and struck out 74 times. His home runs, RBI, and batting average would always be impressive. So were his strikeouts—almost as much fun and excitement for fans as the drives into the seats.

Sluggers who hit long home runs usually strike out often. It is a part of their drama. It is the anticipation of the event, the huge home run or the disappointing strikeout, which brings fans to the park.

Clearly, Mantle, with his potential for those huge home runs or those discouraging strikeouts, would always be a draw.

The Yankees were in a tough pennant race with Cleveland in the final days of the 1951 season. Allie Reynolds pitched a no-hitter for the second time in 1951 as the Yankees pushed ahead of Cleveland. Vic Raschi won the second game of a doubleheader, and the Yankees wrapped up their third straight pennant under Stengel.

The World Series would wait a few more days while the New York Giants and the Brooklyn Dodgers settled their pennant race. The season had ended in a tie, and they were scheduled for a three-game playoff.

The Giants won the first game on Monday. The Dodgers came back behind relief pitcher Clem Labine, thrown in as an emergency starter to win the second game on Tuesday. Now the third game in the Polo Grounds was set.

Brooklyn led 4-1 going into the last of the ninth with Don Newcombe, the big right-hander, besting Sal Maglie. Larry Jansen, the other New York Giants ace, pitched the Brooklyn ninth.

The Giants got a run, had men on second and third with one out. Brooklyn brought in Ralph Branca, who had allowed a homer to Bobby Thomson in the first game.

Branca faced Thomson again. Branca had been a very successful pitcher for the Dodgers, winning 21 games at the age of twenty-one, one of the youngest players in baseball history to record that feat.

Now he was facing Thomson with the pennant on the line. He got a quick strike on Thomson. The next pitch was another fastball on the inside part of the plate. Thomson hit a low line drive to left field.

"Sink, sink, sink," Branca recalled saying as the ball headed to the wall.

Dodger left fielder Andy Patko leaned against the fence only 254 feet from home plate. The ball was over his head and into the seats for a home run.

The game was broadcast and telecast only locally. The cry of Giants announcer Russ Hodges survives to this day. *"The Giants win the pennant, the Giants win the pennant, the Giants win the pennant!"*

Now the Giants would face the Yankees in the 1951 World Series. This was the fourth time in five years that a New York team would be in the World Series and the third time in those five years that representatives of both leagues in the World Series would be from New York.

The Yankees had beaten Brooklyn in seven games in 1947 and five games in 1949, Stengel's first year as field boss.

Stengel announced his lineup for the game against the Giants on Thursday, October 4, 1951.

Mickey Mantle, sixteen days shy of his twentieth birthday, would lead off for the Yankees and play right field. Phil Rizzuto would bat second at shortstop, Hank Bauer would play left field and bat third, and Joe DiMaggio would bat fourth and play center field. Then came Yogi Berra behind the plate, Gil McDougald at third base, Jerry Coleman at second, Joe Collins at first base, and Allie Reynolds as the starting pitcher.

The Giants, still high from their pennant triumph, won the opener, 5-1 behind a cagey left-hander named Dave Koslo.

The hero of the game was Monte Irvin, a black outfielder who had four hits and stole home for the first time in World Series play since 1928.

Forty-five years after that play, Yogi Berra would repeat the same words that he had repeated to umpire Bill Summers that October afternoon. "He was out."

Mantle drew a couple of walks off Koslo as the veteran Giants pitcher took charge of the big guys on the club. He allowed only seven hits with McDougald getting a double for the only extra base blow.

Eddie Lopat beat the Giants the next day, but Mantle didn't even notice. He was in a hospital bed at Lenox Hill Hospital when the game ended. It would impact his life and career for the rest of his days.

DiMaggio, playing his final season and final Series, was a step or two slower than he had been in his younger days. He still had that same graceful stride, but wasn't getting to as many balls in the gap as he had before.

Nothing is more difficult for a manager than dealing with a player at the end of his career. It is hard to bench him or move him. Some managers choose to ride out the difficulties until the star gets the message himself and quits. It happened with Ted Williams, Stan Musial, Willie Mays, Hank Aaron, and Al Kaline. It was more difficult with DiMaggio.

His standing with the Yankees was too important to be changed by the manager. After all, he had played with Gehrig, anchored all those pennant winners, and was not that old at thirty-six. Ruth had played until he was forty.

Mantle got a bunt single, his first of 59 World Series hits, in the third inning of the second game off Larry Jansen. Rizzuto pushed a bunt single to third, and McDougald singled to right for a run.

Willie Mays led off for the Giants in the sixth inning. He had joined the team at the end of May, struggled early, then soon established himself with a .274 average and 20 home runs. He was nervous as could be while he waited in the on-deck circle before Thomson homered to win the pennant.

"I was just a kid then and that was some pressure. I prayed for him to get the game over without me having to bat. By the time the Series came I was relaxed. Nobody could take it away from us now, because we had beaten Brooklyn and won the pennant," he said.

Lopat threw a slow curve to Mays, and he hit it off the end of the bat to right center field.

"In those days I hit most of my long balls to right center. I wasn't pulling enough then and the pitchers all worked me outside," Mays said.

The ball sliced to the spot between Mantle in right and DiMaggio in center. DiMaggio, accustomed to catching everything he could get his hands on, moved gracefully for the ball. Mantle, thinking DiMaggio had slowed down significantly, raced hard to his right.

"I got it," yelled DiMaggio with confidence.

The Yankee Clipper's call was in contrast to the one made by a huge Los Angeles Dodgers outfielder, Frank Howard, who moved to a fly ball and called off his center fielder, Willie Davis, by shouting, "I'll try it."

DiMaggio caught the ball easily. At that instant Mantle had slowed up and caught his right foot in an exposed drain. He went down hard.

The Stadium crowd was silent as Mantle lay on the ground. DiMaggio comforted him while the Yankees trainer, Gus Mauch, raced out to the injured youngster. A stretcher was called for. Mantle was lifted on to the stretcher and carried off the field.

He was operated on the next day for torn ligaments in his knee, an injury that slowed his running, caused excess pressure on his left leg, and probably shortened his career.

As a result of that injury, the most common sight in the Yankee clubhouse before games was of Mantle wrapping his legs with bandages for support. It is why most sportswriters like myself remember interviewing the top of Mantle's head for so many years. He was always sitting on that clubhouse stool, wrapping one leg or the other.

Mantle's father went with Mickey to Lenox Hill Hospital. Mutt Mantle looked pale and weak. Years of working the mines had damaged his body. He was examined at Lenox Hill while Mickey was being prepared for surgery. The next day Mutt Mantle's results came back. He had incurable Hodgkin's disease and would be gone in a little more than seven months. He was only thirty-nine years old.

Mickey Mantle spent that winter of 1951 depressed over his father's condition and concerned about his own.

He married his high school sweetheart, Merlyn Johnson, a few days before Christmas. Mantle had turned twenty just two months earlier, and Merlyn was nineteen. It was not an unusually early age for newlyweds in that dreary part of Oklahoma.

Mantle had bought a new home for his parents with his World Series earnings. He also rented an apartment nearby for his new bride and himself. He sat through most of the winter, with his knee in a split, watching television, drinking beer, and thinking about his father.

He had made it through his rookie season. Now he could settle in as a Yankee—most importantly, as the center fielder of the Yankees since DiMaggio had announced his retirement officially the previous November.

Mantle would be expected to compete for the center field spot in the spring of 1952 with another talented youngster, Jackie Jensen, and a journeyman ballplayer, Bob Cerv.

Casey Stengel, who had fallen in love with Mantle's raw power in the spring of 1951, knew that as long as he, Casey, had anything to say around the Yankees, this youngster would be his center fielder. Stengel, in his wisdom, already understood that Mantle was a rare talent, a baseball find, a once-in-a-lifetime player.

Stengel knew one thing for sure. Long after he was gone from the Yankees, long after his records were forgotten, Mantle would be part of his legacy. This youngster was like no other player he had ever seen.

"He just might be the best there ever was," Stengel said to a group of reporters that winter.

Mantle sat home in Commerce feeling depression over his shattered knee, sorrow over his dying father, and apprehension about his new challenges in life as a married man at the age of twenty.

He was hardly concerned that winter with his own immortality.

Still a kid, 1955

Hitting His Stride

E lvin *"Mutt" Mantle died of Hodgkin's disease on May 6, 1952. He was thirty-nine years old. Mickey Mantle was twenty.*

"Mickey talked about his father a great deal," said Whitey Ford. "They were incredibly close. I don't think anything ever impacted on his life the way the death of his dad did. Mickey was certain, like his dad, he would die early."

The prospect of an early death matured Mantle and frightened him. It colored every aspect of his life. It made him more callous and more careless. An edge of sadness, bitterness, and anger stayed with Mickey for the rest of his life.

After Mutt Mantle's death, Casey Stengel became a much more significant person in Mickey's life.

Stengel had broken into baseball in 1912 as an outfielder with the Brooklyn Dodgers. He had managed to hang on for fourteen years in the big leagues with modest talent. He had played with or against most of the great players of his time—Ty Cobb, Babe Ruth, Walter Johnson, and Rogers Hornsby. He'd managed Joe DiMaggio for three seasons. He'd managed against Ted Williams. Still, he had never seen anyone like Mantle.

Stengel always knew that Mantle could be the monument by which he, Stengel, would be measured. He never stopped bragging about him to the press, and he never stopped feeling emotional about him personally or when speaking with his wife, Edna.

Mantle was the son Casey never had, especially after Mantle lost his own father.

Stengel was smart enough not to push Mantle past his breaking point. In the spring of 1952, he told the press that Mantle would compete with Jackie Jensen, an All American football player turned baseball player, and burly Bob Cerv for the center field job.

It eased the burden on Mantle.

The home runs continued to come. Mantle hit 13 as a rookie and 23 in 1952 in his second season. One of his 1951 homers was off future Hall of Famer Satchel Paige, the great star of the old Negro Leagues. In 1952 he hit home runs off future Hall of Famers Bob Lemon, Hal Newhouser, and Early Wynn.

The home runs often brought smiles and giddiness in the clubhouse. But during a game, players showed little emotion on the field. Mantle had a habit of hitting a home run, even a huge one, and immediately staring at the dirt as he left home plate. He would jog the bases, head down, rarely making eye contact with the third baseman or third base coach as he rounded the bag. He hardly ever tipped his cap as he crossed home plate.

In the 1950s players shook hands at home plate in modest congratulations. There were no high fives or low fives, no leaps into the air, no public exuberance. If anything considered out of line was done, for any attempt to embarrass a rattled pitcher, the batter would pay. A baseball might hit him in the ribs on the next pitch.

In an eight-team league, with only eighty pitching jobs available, embarrassing a pitcher was to be avoided at all costs. Early Wynn was well known as a hard thrower who would lean a batter back or maybe hit him after a home run.

"Wynn would hit his own mother if she dug in at the plate on him," a sportswriter wrote of Burly Gus.

"Why not," responded Wynn. "She's a tough hitter."

By the middle of 1952, it was obvious to most American League pitchers that Mantle could be pitched to low and away, or high and inside, especially when he was batting from the left side. If the pitcher's control was slightly off, if the pitch was more to the center of the plate where Mantle could stretch his arms, the ball might wind up in the third deck at Yankee Stadium.

Even in batting practice, it became a contest of sorts for players to compete with Mantle for distance in their drives. It became a daily game.

"Nobody could drive a ball like Mickey," said Hank Bauer. "I'd hit one in the upper deck in batting practice and Mickey would follow me with a ball about thirty or forty rows higher. Then he would just laugh like hell."

The Yankees won the pennant again in 1952. The Brooklyn Dodgers were their opponents in the World Series. It seemed the World Series was a private New York show for the past few years. It had been the Yankees against the Dodgers in 1947, again in 1949, and now again in 1952. The Yankees had beaten the New York Giants in 1951. Somehow Philadelphia had snuck into that monopoly in 1950. They were dispatched in four games.

The Yankees had to go seven games in 1952 against Brooklyn before they could lock up the Series.

Billy Martin made a great play, coming in from second base to catch a pop fly by Jackie Robinson in the seventh game in Brooklyn. The bases were loaded, and the count was 3-2. First baseman Joe Collins froze on the pop-up, and Martin raced in to make the catch at his knees, with a dramatic lunge. It became the most memorable catch of a pop-up in baseball history—a story Billy Martin loved to tell to anyone, anytime.

"Nobody wanted it," Martin would say, "but I had to get it."

"He damn near ran out of his uniform to catch it," said Casey Stengel.

Martin and Mantle had developed an incredible bond by then. Whitey Ford was off in the service, so Mantle and Martin were together as roommates during the season. They were traveling companions as well as pals at home and during the off-season.

Martin, a journeyman player at best, was loud, brash, and constantly obscene. He enjoyed a good time, a glass of Scotch, or a willing woman as much as he enjoyed a winning game.

Mantle seemed only to tag along, to follow Billy everywhere, laughing at his outrageous conduct and reveling in the way Billy shouted down the press and opposing players. Martin had the kind of brash personality, confidence, and bravado that Mantle could only dream about. It was all in the genes.

When Whitey Ford returned from service and rejoined the Yankees in 1954, Mantle and Martin had been remarkably close for those two seasons.

Ford was never as comfortable with Martin as Mickey was. Mickey was close to Billy and grew close to Whitey. Billy worshiped Mickey, but tolerated Whitey and actually felt a little jealous of Mantle's devotion for his pitching friend. Something about two's company and three's a crowd was at play here.

Mantle batted .311 in 1952 and hit 23 homers. He also struck out 111 times to lead the league in that category.

Each strikeout caused a massive depression and some wild outbursts of temper. It was impossible, especially in those early days of his career, for Mantle to accept any kind of failure. Sluggers strike out. It is why they are sluggers. They swing hard on every pitch. Nobody ever swung harder than Mantle. If they guess wrong on the pitch location, they will look bad striking out. Nobody looked worse more often than Mantle.

"It's all because I try and hit the hell out of the ball every time I'm up," he said.

There is so much at work here, so much machismo, so much peer pressure. Once a hitter is advertised as a slugger, he will be measured by the distance of his home runs.

One home run early in 1953 would change Mantle's life forever.

Chuck Stobbs was a journeyman left-hander with the Washington Senators in 1953. He had broken in with Boston in 1947, had been traded to the Chicago White Sox in 1952, then came to the Senators in 1953. He lasted fifteen years in the big leagues, finishing with a record of 107-130. He became famous—or infamous—for one pitch to Mantle.

On April 17, 1953, the Yankees played the Washington Senators at Griffith Stadium in Washington. Martin led off the inning with a single, was sacrificed to second, and moved to third on a ground out. Mantle was the next hitter.

"Stobbs had a nice, easy overhand motion," said Mantle. "I had gotten him once the year before for a homer. He threw hard but not too hard. He also had good control. He was always around the plate."

On a 1-0 pitch, Stobbs threw a fastball over the middle of the plate, hard but not too hard, straight, and just where Mantle, batting right-handed, liked a pitch.

Mantle's split-second swing connected against the 85 to 88 mile per hour fastball. The ball rocketed off Mantle's bat. It headed quickly for the left field fence, cleared the fence by several feet, grazed a scoreboard sign, and continued on a rising arch as it escaped the ballpark.

Red Patterson, the Yankees publicity director, jumped from his seat in the press box.

"Whew, I've never seen one like that," he said.

Patterson had worked for the Brooklyn Dodgers before coming to the Yankees. He knew how to manufacture a story out of very little. Mantle, by now, had hit 36 big-league home runs, some of them for enor-

Mickey, with wife Merlyn, horsin' around with his two boys at home in River Edge, New Jersey, 1955

mous distances. This one, on the face of it, may or may not have been his longest at the time. Patterson, sharp in the ways of the journalistic world, left no doubt about it. *This* was a home run to be immortalized.

He left the press box, walked down a ramp of Griffith Stadium, bought himself a hot dog and a beer, stayed away from the sportswriters for about ten minutes, and then returned.

"Red was an idea guy but not a physical guy," said Harold Rosenthal, a sportswriter covering the game for the *New York Herald Tribune*. "He wasn't about to walk down the entire length of the ball park, leaving the field, chase a kid down a street and measure a home run. Where the hell would he get a tape measure? It was all a promotion."

Patterson, a tough-talking, confident, red-faced Irishman, walked back into the press box and announced, "We measured it. Some kid saw it bounce outside. The ball went 565 feet."

Sportswriters rarely question the statistical information offered to them by representatives of the team. They may question an injury or a trade detail, but never a number.

Patterson said it traveled 565 feet. Every sportswriter wrote that the huge home run traveled 565 feet.

The next day's newspapers were filled with the heroics of the blast. Stobbs was questioned in depth about the pitch and asked if he was embarrassed that the ball had been hit so far off him.

"The kid's a good hitter. What the hell's the difference? It's just a home run. It only counts for one run," he said that day.

In 1995 he was asked again about the famous home run.

"It was all exaggerated, everybody knew that," he said from his retirement home in Sarasota, Florida. He had finished his pitching career and then worked for Kansas City and Cleveland as a pitching instructor. "Nobody ever talks about the times I struck Mickey out. He was a strong kid. If you made a mistake, he could drive it on you. If you made a mistake on a little guy, he hit a single."

Stobbs said the distance attributed to Mantle's hit never really bothered him.

"Actually, it helped me. At least once a year somebody asks me about it. When Mickey died, a lot of people asked me about it. My son, Charles, was on a business trip to New York and went into Mantle's restaurant. Moose Skowron and Hank Bauer [former Mantle teammates] were there. They asked him about it. The kid is only twenty-eight," Stobbs said.

He remembered one other thing about the home run.

"After the fuss in the papers the next day, somebody from our club put the ball up on the scoreboard just where Mickey had grazed it. Our manager, Bucky Harris, went crazy over that. He made them take it right down."

Mantle had been responsible, via Patterson, for adding a significant phrase to baseball: "tape measure home run."

Patterson certainly didn't carry a tape measure around in his pocket in 1953, but until the end of his days he swore that he had acquired one on his walk outside the park.

No matter. The expression caught on. All huge home runs were for ever after called tape measure home runs and compared to Mantle's. In the 1990s, baseball developed an actual computer method of measuring the distances for home runs. Even with computer analysis, no home run has ever reached 565 feet. The truth is that Mantle never hit one that far, either.

The Patterson creation had separated Mantle from the crowd. Al Rosen, Gus Zernial, Larry Doby, and Ted Williams were the home run kings of the league in the early 1950s. Each had hit huge home runs. None had hit a tape measure job, and none would be watched for the distance of their drives as Mantle was after that day in April.

The 1953 season was another historic season for the Yankees. They won their fifth straight pennant under Casey Stengel and went on to win their fifth straight World Series, again against the Brooklyn Dodgers.

The Yankees won the Series in six games. Mantle hit two home runs, including a grand slam off Dodger right-hander Monk Meyer. He also struck out eight times, including five in a row.

Mantle was almost always a feast or a famine for the fans. Huge home runs earned him cheers. Those strikeouts had fans booing his whiffs all the way to the dugout. Some were still angry that he was not DiMaggio. Others expected super results from each at bat. Still others were jealous of a kid getting that much attention and at the same time avoiding the draft with an ailment that hardly seemed to impact on his baseball.

"Sometimes I would do so badly it would make me cry," Mantle once said.

He always seemed to take his failures more to heart. He never seemed able to enjoy his successes as much. Some of this was due to his intense nature. Some was simply the unquestioned mathematics of the game—a sport where even the best fail approximately two out of every three times at bat.

Billy Martin defied those classic odds in the 1953 Series with 12 hits in 24 at bats for a .500 average. Casey Stengel was beside himself with joy as Martin shone.

Perhaps the most exciting game of the Series occurred in game three when Carl Erskine struck out 14 Yankees for a World Series record. He got Mantle and first baseman Joe Collins four times each in that game.

Ballplayers love to needle each other, second guess the manager, and pass the blame of failure on to others. First baseman Johnny Mize was one of the best at that.

Erskine had started the first game for Brooklyn and was hit hard. He was gone in the second inning as the Yankees won 9-5. They won the next day 4-2. Brooklyn manager Charlie Dressen, short of pitching, brought Erskine back after only one full day of rest for game three.

This time the curveballing right-hander from Anderson, Indiana, one of the game's true gentlemen and a successful banker in later life, had his stuff. He was getting the Yankees out with his sinking curveball. He tied the Series strikeout record of 13 when he retired left-handed pinch hitter Don Bollweg.

At each strikeout Mize, sitting on the Yankee bench, yelled to his teammates, "Make him bring it up." That meant that hitters, at Mize's instructions, should lay off the sinking curveball and wait for the high fastball.

"Make him bring it up, make him bring it up," Mize yelled at Mantle, Collins, and Gene Woodling as they struck out on Erskine's curve.

Finally, Mize had his own chance as he batted for pitcher Vic Raschi with one out in the ninth inning. He swung and missed at the third strike, a ball that bounced in the dirt for the record-breaking 14th strikeout of the game.

"Make him bring it up," Martin whispered to Mantle.

Mantle hit only .208 in that Series but had two home runs. The tape measures were kept in the closet.

Billy Martin was in the Army most of the 1954 and 1955 seasons. Ford was back from his Army service, and he and Mickey grew closer than ever.

Ford could always get Mantle out of a blue period. If the strikeouts were outweighing the home runs, Ford would ease Mickey through it.

"Most of all we didn't talk about it," said Ford. "We would go out, have a few pops and kid around. By that time Mickey usually forgot if he had a good day or a bad day in the park."

The Cleveland Indians won 111 games in 1954. The Yankees winning streak was over. For the first October since he joined the team, Mantle was at home in Oklahoma early that fall.

He spent most of his time in local bars, kidding with old friends, going on hunting trips away from home, spending a few days fishing, playing a little basketball with old pals.

It was the routine most young ballplayers follow. They are away all summer playing baseball. They spend most of the off-season staying away from home and counting the days until spring training.

Mickey Mantle paid all expenses. Merlyn Mantle raised their children.

When Mantle retired after the 1968 season, I asked what he thought he would miss most about not playing any more.

"Just hanging around with the guys," he said.

Maybe family life is not what drives ballplayers. Sometimes the wives may be just as happy not to see them all the time. Hazel Weiss, the wife of Yankee general manager George Weiss, put it best after Weiss was retired by the Yankees and before he moved over to run the New York Mets.

"I married George for better or for worse," she said. "Not for lunch."

Weiss had been around baseball since the early 1920s. He had been the operator of a team in Hartford, Connecticut Then he was a farm director with the Yankees before becoming the general manager and architect of the championship teams in the 1950s.

It was Weiss who had brought Stengel to the Yankees in the 1949 season. It was Weiss who made the deals, brought the young players along, and developed the Yankee dynasty. It was Weiss who controlled every personnel move around the Yankees for owners Dan Topping, a playboy heir to an inherited fortune, and Del Webb, a real estate magnate with major operations in California and Arizona.

A major social dynamic was at work around the Yankees by 1954. Branch Rickey, the Brooklyn Dodger general manager, had signed Jackie Robinson in 1945, sent him to the Montreal farm club in 1946, and brought him up to the big leagues in 1947.

All other baseball owners voted against the move to integrate when it was presented at a major-league council.

Commissioner Albert B. "Happy" Chandler, a former Kentucky governor and senator, approved Rickey's move.

Robinson became the first Negro in big-league baseball since before the turn of the century. Robinson, despite more pressure than any player ever experienced in making a big-league club, was named the National League Rookie of the Year in 1947. He would go on to a brilliant career with Brooklyn and was later elected to baseball's Hall of Fame. His plaque in Cooperstown advertises his baseball skills. It has not one word on it about his race or his contribution to integrating the game.

Negro players still made baseball owners nervous—as late as 1962 when Robinson was inducted into the Hall of Fame in Cooperstown, New York.

After Robinson, the Cleveland Indians, under Bill Veeck, signed Larry Doby. Soon most other big-league clubs would have black players.

The Yankees had none through 1954.

Weiss, the man in charge, said there were no qualified Negro players. He wanted someone who would play well for the Yankees and uphold the team's image, as Weiss saw it. Weiss was simply an old-fashioned bigot who saw Negro players as less than whites. It was an attitude most of the Yankee executives, including owners Topping and Webb, shared.

One black player, Vic Power, a flashy first baseman from Puerto Rico, got close. He was a Yankee farm hand. Then he was traded to Philadelphia in 1954.

Black groups, led by the National Association for the Advancement of Colored People, picketed Yankee Stadium. Black sportswriters in the black press lambasted the Yankees for their stand. Boycotts were threatened. Liberals, led by the *New York Post*, clamored for a black Yankee.

The Yankees had one promising Negro player in the organization. He was a catcher at their Toronto farm club by the name of Elston Howard.

Howard, a St. Louis native, made the club in spring training in 1955. He could catch, play first base, and play the outfield. He could hit good pitching, and he could hit with power. He was a gentleman in every sense of the word, and he wasn't abrasive, a militant about race, or a drinker—traits that Weiss had feared when he considered playing a Negro.

What he couldn't do on a ball field was run fast.

"When I finally get a black player," said Casey Stengel, "I get the only one who can't run."

Stengel had been born in 1890 in Kansas City, Missouri. Slavery was gone only a quarter of a century by then. Stengel had the racial attitudes possessed by most nineteenth-century Americans.

The Yankee manager soon learned to respect and admire Howard, who played hard, kept his mouth shut, dressed neatly, avoided controversy, and honored the Yankee uniform.

Until Howard's premature death in 1980, he remained one of the most admired players among teammates and executives.

In 1955 it didn't take long for the Yankee players—Mantle, Ford, Martin, Berra, and others—to accept Howard into their team.

Howard had proven that he could play baseball well. He had proven he could go along, upset no one, and cause no fuss. Unlike Jackie Robinson, who saw every slight and every indignity as being racially motivated, Howard accepted everything with ease. His teammates respected him as a player and a gentleman. Mantle, only twenty-three that spring in 1955, accepted Howard quickly.

Their relationship was civil, if not personal. Mantle rented a beach

Mantle bears down—during batting
practice—before the 1955 World
Series at Yankee Stadium.

house in the spring with Merlyn and the kids. Howard stayed with his wife, Arlene, in a small rented apartment in St. Petersburg's black neighborhood.

It would be a painful reminder that eight years after Jackie Robinson's arrival in the big leagues, integration was still not fully implemented.

Integration would not come to St. Petersburg until the early 1960s when some of the members of the St. Louis Cardinals, who also trained in St. Petersburg, Florida, refused to accept segregated housing conditions. They moved into the downtown St. Louis Cardinals hotel with their teammates. Players such as Bill White, later to be the National League president; Curt Flood, who would be instrumental in fighting baseball free agency; and Bob Gibson, a Hall of Famer, led the move.

Stengel had been disappointed in the team's showing in 1954. Even though the Yankees won 103 ball games, the most ever under Stengel, they were never in the race.

But the Yankees came back to win again in 1955. Mantle had another big year with a .306 average, 99 runs batted in, and his first home run title with 37.

"I still was striking out too much [97 times that year] but I was walking more [a league-leading 113 times] so that was a good sign," he said.

His popularity was growing. He had finally become the dominant player on the team. Hordes of youngsters waited for him outside the gates of Yankee Stadium after each game, but he rarely acknowledged their presence. Instead he rushed off with a teammate or friend to a downtown Manhattan restaurant—Shor's, Danny's Hideaway or P. J. Clarke's—for a quick meal and a lot of drinks. There might be a nightclub stop after that, a hotel party, or a visit to a teammate's home.

Merlyn and the boys were rarely in New York during those times. Mantle would occasionally rent a home in New Jersey for them all during the summer months. More often he would suggest Merlyn stay back in Oklahoma, avoid the burden of caring for the kids in New York, and allow him to party with his pals.

By now Billy Martin had been divorced by his wife, Lois, and he rarely had time for his infant daughter, Kelly. New York had too many bright lights for these guys to see.

In 1955 Mantle's fame was such that he could hardly go anywhere in New York City without being recognized, fussed over, and cheered. The same fans who would boo a strikeout at a clutch time at a Stadium game would cheer Mantle when he walked into Shor's.

Mantle felt uncomfortable around fawning fans. His ego didn't need that. He was comfortable with a few close friends, teammates mostly, and the few Yankee officials he admired, especially Stengel.

He was comfortable in the clubhouse with clubhouse man Pete Sheehy.

Sheehy had arrived at Yankee Stadium in 1926 as a fan brought in to help in the locker room. He worked his way up to clubhouse custodian and was honored with the Yankee clubhouse named for him after his death.

Pete Sheehy and his long time assistant Pete Previte, known to the players as Big Pete and Little Pete, would arrive at the clubhouse before a day game at seven o'clock in the morning.

On rare occasions, Mantle would show up in the clubhouse by himself, usually after a long night, take a nap on the training table, and wake up before any of the other players or manager Casey Stengel, also an early arriver, showed up at the clubhouse.

By the middle 1950s Mantle had a ritual when he came to the park. He hung up his clothes, put on his undershorts and undershirt, put a jock over his shorts, and began bandaging his legs. He had pain from his knees down to his ankles by that time, almost every day. The only way he could relieve the tension in his legs was to wrap his legs with thick bandages, sometimes as high as his thighs.

Sheehy, who was a quiet man and knew the rules of clubhouse etiquette ("What you hear here stays here," read a Yankee sign) would often notice Mantle struggling with the bandages.

"I can't believe he can get out there every day," he once told me. "I've never seen a player in such pain."

Through it all, the injuries, the pressures of his status, the demands on his time, Mantle performed.

The Yankees now prepared for the 1955 World Series. Their opponents, as so often before, were again the Brooklyn Dodgers.

The Dodgers were having one of their finest seasons ever. They had opened the season with a 10-game winning streak and were 21-1 after 22 games. They won the pennant by 13 games over the Milwaukee Braves.

Brooklyn had grown incredibly frustrated with the October Classic failures. Jackie Robinson, Roy Campanella, Duke Snider, Carl Furillo, Carl Erskine, the heart of the team, were all growing old. If the Dodgers didn't beat the Yankees soon, it might never happen.

Many Brooklyn fans felt that this was the best Brooklyn team ever. It was now or never for Brooklyn.

The Yankees won the first two games in Yankee Stadium. Depression in Brooklyn was high as the teams moved across the East River for the third game in Ebbets Field.

Mantle, suffering another knee injury, was unable to play the first two games. It didn't seem to matter when the Yankees won 6-5 and 4-2.

By the third game Mantle had improved a bit. He was still limping painfully, but was in Stengel's lineup against a young left-hander from upstate New York, Johnny Podres.

Podres, twenty-three years old that September 30, 1955, was a cocky kid with a hard fastball and a terrific change-up. He had good control for a left-hander and had been a reliable starter.

"I was injured in a freak accident in late August," Podres said. "I was in the outfield taking fungo balls when the batting cage hit me. The guys pushing the cage to center field didn't see me coming and pushed the cage right into me. It cut my leg and ankle severely. I had a dozen stitches and missed about five weeks of the season. I got back in the last week and didn't know if I would make the Series."

Manager Walter Alston, who had missed winning in his first year as skipper in 1954 when Leo Durocher's New York Giants beat Brooklyn, picked Podres for the third game.

The Yankees got only seven hits off Podres, including Mantle's fifth World Series home run, in an 8-3 loss to Brooklyn.

The Dodgers went up three games to two after Clem Labine won in relief and rookie right-hander Roger Craig, with relief help again from Labine, won 5-3.

The Yankees took the sixth game behind Ford's four hitter, 5-1. It all came down to the seventh game at Yankee Stadium on October 4, 1955.

Podres was the starter again for Brooklyn. Mantle, suffering severe leg pain, could not make the starting lineup that day. He sat on the bench forlornly as Podres shut the Yankees out 2-0. Brooklyn got its first World Series triumph ever. The borough of Brooklyn went wild with joy.

Elston Howard, the Negro rookie, was the final batter in the game. He hit a roller to shortstop. Pee Wee Reese, the veteran Dodger who had been going through World Series agonies with Brooklyn since 1941, fielded it cleanly. He threw a little low to first base. Gil Hodges, the big Brooklyn first baseman, caught the ball for the final out.

Years later Hodges was managing the New York Mets. His team was in San Francisco. At three o'clock in the morning, Hodges was fast asleep in his hotel room at the Jack Tar. The phone rang. Hodges answered sleepily. It was Don Hoak, the third baseman on that Brooklyn team.

"I'm here with Pee Wee," he said in a drunken voice.

"It bounced," Hodges said and hung up the phone.

It had been a long running gag that Pee Wee had choked on the final out of the 1955 Series, bounced his throw, and had been saved by Hodges.

Hodges had always gone along with the gag.

"It never bounced," insisted Pee Wee. "I had waited too long for that play to let the ball bounce."

Brooklyn finally had the Series it had craved so dearly. The Yankees knew that they would be back again in 1956. It hardly mattered. If they were short a player or two for winning the championship, George Weiss and Casey Stengel would take care of all that over the winter.

Before the next season, the Yankees had one more obligation as a team. They played an exhibition tour in Japan.

Stengel had been in Japan several times in the 1920s and 1930s on exhibition tours. He had given clinics there and had come to admire Japanese baseball. The Japanese played the game with intelligence and discipline, even if they lacked some of the physical strengths of American players.

The Yankees played a dozen games throughout Japan, moving from Tokyo to Yokohama to smaller cities and more remote sites. The players took it all as a joke while the Japanese, only ten years after the end of World War II, tried hard to impress.

Most of the time the Yankees won. The crowds were large and enthusiastic. Stengel entertained the Japanese press as he did the American press. He double-talked his way through Japan. Few understood him. All enjoyed him.

I was a soldier in the United States Army that fall, stationed at Camp Drake outside of Tokyo. I was a part-time sportswriter for *Pacific Stars and Stripes*, the army newspaper, and covered a few games in Tokyo.

I stood next to Mickey Mantle for the first time on a field in Tokyo. He was a couple of years older than I was, but looked many years older to me. He seemed incredibly strong. His hair, cut short, was a very light blonde, and he talked with a twang I had never heard growing up in New York, as he bantered with teammates at the batting cage. I approached him for an interview. He stared at me as if I were from Mars. I had obviously caught him after one of his long nights.

I settled for Billy Martin. He always laughed about it years later when I brought him a copy of the 1955 interview and reminded him he was just a substitute for Mickey.

The Yankees won the game 7-3 that day. Mantle batted only once and struck out. Billy Martin had two singles.

My story ran in *Stars and Stripes* next to a picture of Casey Stengel sitting on the Yankee bench with his head down. He was holding a pair of bedroom slippers in his hand. He had also obviously had a long night before the game.

It's 1956 and Mickey
looks content — for
good reason.

Mickey's Team

*merica was living through one of the sweetest periods of its
history in the middle 1950s.*

President Dwight Eisenhower was a beloved figure
with incredible popular support. He had been a great
hero of World War II, leading the Great Crusade in
Europe. Now he had risen to his country's greatest heights as leader of our nation.

Millions of men and women who had
served in World War II had now completed
school, married, and started families. They
bought homes in the suburbs, worked at
satisfying jobs, and enjoyed life at home.

The leisure industry exploded.

Baseball, especially in New York City,
was at its glorious peak. Between 1951 and
1956, New York had two hometown teams
in the World Series every year except 1954.

Mickey Mantle was the player much of
the country focused on when they thought of
the joys of baseball.

Mickey launches one in the 1956 World Series against rival Brooklyn.

By early 1956, Mickey was one of America's most instantly recognizable figures. His name dominated sports stories from early February to late October, day after day, game after game. There was an unending torrent of information and trivia concerning his every move, as writers sought to appease the public's intense interest in their hero.

Every winter he returned to Commerce, Oklahoma. That only served to solidify his image. Returning home each fall kept him grounded. It kept him connected with his past. As famous and successful as he was on the ball field, he remained humble, unassuming, and unpretentious off of it. America liked that about him. He could play ball, raise a little hell in his off hours, be fined by general manager George Weiss for missing a curfew—but he always returned to his roots after the season's end.

"I couldn't wait for spring training to begin each year," he once said, "and I couldn't wait to get home after the Series ended."

In the spring of 1956, as he started his sixth season with the Yankees, he seemed more mature, more confident, and more relaxed than he had ever been.

"I think the pressure of living up to those early expectations was gone by then," said Whitey Ford. "He could relax and just let his ability take over."

Mantle started fast that year and never slowed down. He began hitting home runs at a rapid pace. Late into the summer he was ahead of Babe Ruth's record pace of 1927. Charts began appearing in newspapers comparing Mantle's numbers with Ruth's. Ruth had 17 homers in the last month of the 1927 season during which he hit a record 60 home runs.

Mantle hit only five homers in September of 1956. That ended the chase.

Still, he batted .353 to beat Ted Williams out in the batting race. (Williams finished with a .345 mark.) Mantle led the league with 130 runs batted in and won the home run title with 52 homers.

He was named the American League Most Valuable Player that year and won the Hickok Belt, symbolic of the most successful athlete in America.

The Yankees came back in the fall of 1956 to avenge the 1955 Series loss to Brooklyn. They won in seven games. Don Larsen pitched baseball's only perfect World Series game that fall. Mantle's catch of a fierce line drive hit by Gil Hodges helped save the game.

There was one touch of reality that hit Mantle that summer. It had no direct bearing on his life, but it impacted him emotionally.

On Old Timers Day, with Joe DiMaggio suiting up in the Yankees clubhouse for his annual appearance, shortstop Phil Rizzuto was called into manager Stengel's office.

Rizzuto had been the Yankee shortstop since 1941, except for the three years he missed in navy service during World War II. He stood five feet, six inches tall, weighed only 150 pounds but could play his position as well as anyone in the game. He was a wonderful bunter and a decent hitter. In 1950 he had batted .324 and won the American League Most Valuable Player title.

He was the object of affection and endless practical jokes around the Yankees. He was afraid of just about everything—lightning, insects, squirmy animals, noises, or things in his food.

The Yankee players, especially Martin and Mantle, loved to fill his glove with caterpillars, dead mice, or half-eaten hot dogs. Fake snakes were bought on every road trip and placed in Rizzuto's glove, locker, or pants.

"I think they got a kick out of hearing me howl," said Rizzuto.

Ballplayers admire physical power and those with enormous skills. But they also respect players who can perform above their ability when it counts. Rizzuto was clearly one of those players—a wonderful shortstop who performed his best in the toughest spots. In 1994 it earned him Hall of Fame recognition.

Rizzuto had become a backup shortstop to Gil McDougald by the summer of 1956. As the Yankees prepared to solidify their team for the upcoming World Series against Brooklyn, Weiss and Stengel agreed they were short one left-handed bat. They obtained veteran Enos Slaughter, who had played for them earlier and been sent to Kansas City. Now they brought him back and needed to clear a roster spot.

Rizzuto was called into Stengel's office. Weiss sat nearby silently in a cushioned chair.

"Who should we drop to make room for Slaughter?" Stengel asked the veteran shortstop.

Rizzuto suggested a pitcher, a backup catcher, or another outfielder.

"Then I finally got the message it was me they were dropping," he said. "I couldn't believe it."

He was hitting only .231 and had batted just .195 a couple of years before. He was almost thirty-nine years old. He still couldn't believe it. Ballplayers are the last to know when they are finished.

If any one moment hardened Mantle's attitude about salary struggles and negotiations, it was Rizzuto's callous release.

"That really hurt me, to see Phil released like that," Mantle said years later. "I knew then if it happened to him, it could happen to anybody. It could happen to me."

By 1956 Mantle was as big a star as the likes of Doris Day, here with Mel Allen (left), Mickey, and Hank Bauer.

The reality, cruelty, and insensitivity in baseball was driven home further one day as Mantle leaned against the railing of the stands, chatting with Claire Ruth, Babe Ruth's widow.

"Babe wanted to manage in '34," she told him. "Instead, he got a pink release slip." The widow of the game's greatest player and most popular draw looked at the young Yankee star.

"Get all you can while you still can," she told him.

Mantle had some bitter negotiations with Weiss through the years. It often took a plea from Lee MacPhail, the Yankee farm director Mantle trusted, for a log jam on salary to be broken.

On one occasion, after Weiss refused to budge on a raise Mantle wanted, owner Del Webb called Mantle at home.

"Mickey, come down to Florida," Webb said. "We'll settle it there."

Not many players, not even Mickey Mantle, could say no to the appeal of the owner of the team.

Mantle retired from baseball long before the tight hold owners had on players was broken. That transformation took place through the efforts of Players Association executive director Marvin Miller.

Mantle never made more than $100,000 as a player—the same figure DiMaggio was making when he retired after the 1951 season. This was also well before the rules of free agency changed and tough agents negotiated big contracts for players.

While Mantle may have been upset about some of his salary negotiations with Weiss, he never carried it over onto the field. Stengel had a lot to do with that. He bragged about Mantle to the press. He also encouraged him to be a tough negotiator for himself. Stengel had his own history of tough negotiating going back more than half a century. It was a game on the field, but it was all business off the field.

Mantle had another big year in 1957. He batted .365. Ted Williams, at thirty-nine, won the batting title with a .388 average. Mantle had 94 runs batted in and 34 home runs.

Years later, at a New York Baseball Writers dinner, Mantle reminisced about his salary negotiations with George Weiss after the 1957 season.

"When I went in to negotiate, I thought I would get a huge raise. He wanted to cut me. He said I didn't win the Triple Crown. I couldn't believe it," Mantle said.

After the dinner at Mantle's restaurant, Mickey talked more about those negotiations.

"Did he really try to cut you after you hit .365, Mick?" I asked him.

Mickey had had a few drinks by then. Obscenities spilled from his lips.

"If he wasn't dead, I'd kill him," Mickey said.

There was one other incident in the summer of 1957 that intensified Mantle's hatred of George Weiss. He broke up Mickey's gang of three.

Billy Martin's birthday was May 16, 1928. Yogi Berra was born May 12, 1925. Mickey and Whitey Ford decided to celebrate both birthdays on a Yankee off-day. The date was set for May 15, 1957.

Mantle and Merlyn met Whitey and Joan Ford for dinner at Danny's Hideaway. They were joined by Hank Bauer and his wife, Yogi and Carmen Berra, Johnny Kucks and his wife, and Billy Martin.

The group enjoyed a wonderful dinner at the Manhattan restaurant and then decided to catch the last show at the Copacabana nightclub, then one of the most famous hangouts in New York City.

Mickey and his Yankee teammates beam after getting revenge against
Brooklyn for 1955 in the 1956 World Series

Mickey moments after discovering he's wrapped up the Triple Crown in 1956, capping one of the most dominant performances in baseball history.

The Triple Crown salute.

Sammy Davis Jr. was performing that night. The group of Yankees had a table near the back. Close to them sat a group of Bronx bowlers celebrating the end of their season.

The bowlers were pretty drunk by the time the Yankee players arrived. They immediately recognized Mantle, Ford, Berra, and the other players. Words were exchanged. Some needling remarks were made about Sammy Davis Jr., many of a racial bent. Tensions increased. One of the bowlers challenged the always combative Billy Martin. He rose from his chair and walked through a side door into the kitchen. Bauer, who had survived mortal combat in the South Pacific as a World War II marine, followed behind him. A loud thud followed.

Yogi Berra has been asked dozens of times about the incident.

"All I know," he said, "is that nobody in our group hit nobody."

Ford, Mantle, Martin, and Kucks swore they hit no one. Bauer suggested the guy was down on the ground when he walked into the kitchen.

"I think a bouncer got him," Bauer said.

Regardless of what the truth of the situation was, the story exploded into the newspapers the following day.

Weiss was enraged. It damaged the Yankee image and could hurt ticket sales. He called all of the players who had been partying that night into his office and fined them.

A month later he struck the final blow. He traded Billy Martin, whom he considered a bad influence, to Kansas City.

Martin bawled like a baby when he was informed of the deal. He blamed his mentor, Casey Stengel, for not protecting him from the trade.

It would take more than five years for Martin to finally forgive Stengel. When Stengel was managing the New York Mets, Martin approached him in a hotel lobby.

"Hi, Case," he said.

"Your ball club did a good thing, hiring you," Stengel said, referring to Billy's new job with the Minnesota Twins.

There was no discussion about the 1957 incident or Billy's trade to Kansas City.

Martin continued to tell Stengel stories for the rest of his life. He attended Stengel's funeral in Glendale, California, in 1975, wept emotionally, drank too much, and passed out on Stengel's bed at his Grandview Avenue home.

Mantle feared that trading Martin away would end their friendship. Billy wouldn't let that happen. While the relationship of most players depends on their being with the same team at the same time, this relationship was different.

Mantle and Martin went out of their way to see each other. They called often, spending as much time together in the off-season as they could manage. They visited whenever they found themselves at the same card shows, banquets, and baseball dinners.

"I always loved him like a brother," Mantle said.

"I never had a brother," said Martin. "I loved him more than a brother."

◆ ◆ ◆

In all the history of sports in America, only a few athletes have crossed that intangible line from idol to icon.

For a very few, John L. Sullivan, Jack Dempsey, Red Grange, Bill Tilden, Bobby Jones, and of course, Babe Ruth, their fame was as significant in the homes of average Americans as it was in the homes of athletic Americans.

How does one measure at what point an athlete crosses that bridge from a sports-page hero to a front-page hero?

A Supreme Court Justice once said, "I can't define obscenity but I know it when I see it."

Most people could not define superstardom, as the term became popular, but they knew it when they saw it. One characteristic of the superstar was transcending one specific area—to have a broad appeal. Whether it was on sports pages or some other area of life, they had to appeal equally to men and women, young and old—the farmer, lawyer, blue-collar worker, and academic alike.

By the middle 1950s, Mickey Mantle had crossed that subtle line.

His was as recognizable a face as there was in America. Whenever he appeared in public, he caused a furor. His arrivals at the Stadium resulted in incredible excitement, and his departures, especially on those home run days, caused innumerable traffic jams.

His mail overwhelmed the Yankee clubhouse, and telephone calls to his room while the club was on the road were never ending.

"About the first thing I did when I arrived at a hotel," he once said, "was shut off the phone."

Somehow, in mysterious ways, pretty, young girls still found Mantle's hotel room. Girls with beautiful faces and attractive figures made better detectives than Dick Tracy.

The Yankees won pennants again in 1957 and 1958. Mantle added another exceptional season in 1957 to his resume and earned his second straight most valuable player title. In 1958 he repeated with another strong season, if a little less than the year before. For the fifth time in six seasons, he batted over .300, with a .304 mark, 97 runs batted in, and a league-leading 42 home runs.

Mel Allen presents Mantle with *Sporting News'* **Player of the Year Award, and American League president Will Harridge performs the same duties on opening day 1957, when Mickey received the award for baseball's Most Valuable Player of 1956.**

At the age of twenty-six, Mantle had two MVP awards, three home run titles, one batting title, one RBI title, and one Triple Crown.

Except perhaps for Eisenhower, he was the most popular person in America, though a kid out of Memphis named Elvis Presley was beginning to make inroads on Mantle's claim to that fame.

Mantle played his first World Series outside New York City in 1957, against the Milwaukee Braves. Hundreds of fans jammed the old Pfister Hotel in downtown Milwaukee, awaiting the Yankees in general and Mantle in particular. Signs of welcome were everywhere. Many of the female fans carried bouquets of flowers they were prepared to offer Mantle and other Yankee favorites. Their home phone numbers were scribbled on perfumed pieces of paper.

All of this went for naught as the Yankee management secretly ensconced the team in a resort hotel called Brown's Lake. Sportswriters stayed in the Pfister Hotel and had to explain that they, too, had no idea where Mantle and his pals were staying.

The Yankee brass, Casey Stengel, Lee McPhail, and George Weiss, are on hand as Mantle signs his 1957 contract, which rewarded him handsomely for 1956.

The Series turned out to be an exciting one, with former Yankee farmhand Lew Burdette winning three games. Warren Spahn, a future Hall of Famer, won the fourth as Milwaukee defeated the Yankees, four games to three.

It was only Stengel's second Series defeat in eight tries. It made him particularly grouchy, as Milwaukee had been one of the places where he had managed. He always wanted to shine in his former places of business.

Mantle batted only .263 in this Series, hit a couple of homers, and struck out only once in six games. He was only able to pinch-hit in the second game and missed the third game entirely after Milwaukee second baseman Red Schoendienst landed on his shoulder after an aborted pick-off play.

Milwaukee hometown boy Tony Kubek, later a successful broadcaster, moved to center field to replace Mantle.

The shoulder bothered Mickey quite a lot in 1958—especially from the left side of the plate. He still managed to play in 150 games, many of which he played in severe pain from a variety of ailments—the ailing shoulder, aching knees, tender hips, and damaged ankles.

He was reaching the years when most baseball players are at peak performance. Babe Ruth was thirty-two years old when he hit his record 60 home runs.

In 1958 one event captured the country's attention concerning the Yankees, manager Casey Stengel and Mantle. It was an appearance in Washington, D.C. on July 8, 1958. Stengel, Mantle, Ted Williams, Stan Musial, and several other players, in town in nearby Baltimore for an All-Star game, were asked to appear before a United States Senate Subcommittee on Antitrust Legislation and Monopoly.

Senator Estes Kefauver of Tennessee had gained a modicum of fame in 1956 as the coonskin-capped vice presidential candidate on the

The media peppers Mickey with questions about his glittering new 1957 contract.

Mantle was now making Babe kind of money.

The natty suit
belies the boy
within.

Democratic ticket under standard-bearer Adlai Stevenson. Now Kefauver was serving as chairman for the subcommittee.

The hearings were called for ten o'clock in the morning so the ballplayers and Stengel could still get to Baltimore in time for the game.

"The room was jammed," said Mary Lavagetto, wife of Cookie Lavagetto, who managed the Washington Senators.

Mary Lavagetto, as a Washington wife, was intensely interested in politics. She was also friendly with Edna and Casey Stengel back home in Glendale, California. She volunteered to sit with Edna while Casey took the stand.

"Casey seemed very jumpy," Mary Lavagetto recalled. "He stood outside the hearing room, chain-smoking, just lighting one cigarette with another before he was called. He was extremely nervous and talked very little. He was dressed so neatly, his hair was plastered down and he appeared as cute as I ever remembered him. I sat there in the front row behind the witness tables with Edna. She was scared to death. We held hands on the bench."

Stengel was twenty-eight days from his sixty-eighth birthday. He wore a gray suit and a new blue tie, which Edna had bought for him only that morning in the hotel lobby men's shop. Stengel held his glasses in his hand, and as Kefauver began to talk, he slipped them on. It was one of the few time he was seen with them in public.

The click of cameras and the flash of light bulbs filled the room.

"Mr. Stengel," began Kefauver, "you are the manager of the New York Yankees. Will you give us, very briefly, your background and your views on this legislation?"

Stengel had been around professional baseball since 1910. This was not the first time he had been interviewed by an intimidating figure of authority.

"Well, I started in professional baseball in 1910," he began speaking softly in a thin, nervous voice. "I have been in professional ball, I would say, for forty-eight years."

At the time of his death in 1975, Stengel had been paid by professional baseball teams steadily for sixty-five years, a record second only to Connie Mack, who owned the Philadelphia Athletics and paid himself.

"I started in the minor leagues with Kansas City. I played as low as Class D ball which was in Shelbyville, Kentucky, and also Class C ball and Class A ball, and I have advanced in baseball as a ball player," continued Stengel.

There was a grin on Kefauver's face as Stengel motored on. His con-

Another celeb wants a moment with the Mick: Movie and TV star Broderick Crawford corners Mantle in the Yankee locker room before a 1957 game.

fidence was now restored. He was in charge of that crowded room, and he rambled on through a half century of baseball.

"I had many years that I was not successful as a ball player as it is a game of skill," he said. "There was no doubt I was discharged by baseball and had to go back to the minor leagues as a manager. I became a major league manager in several cities and was discharged—we call it discharged because there is no question I had to leave."

"By now the smiles and the chuckles had turned into loud laughter," said Mary Lavagetto. "Everyone was laughing so hard it was difficult to hear everything Casey said."

As Stengel paused for breath, Senator John A. Carroll of Kentucky, a committee member, interrupted. "What Senator Kefauver asked you was what, in your opinion, with your forty-eight years of experience, is the need for this legislation in view of the fact that baseball has not been subject to antitrust laws?"

"No," said Stengel.

The audience was howling. Senator Carroll, a serious legislator, then asked a complicated question filled with legalese.

Stengel, who had just performed in Stengelese, a baseball language understood by those of us fortunate enough to be included in his vortex, said "Well, you are going to get me there for about two hours."

Senator Kefauver recognized that information helpful to this proposed legislation was not about to come from the lips of this man. Casey was not one to bite the hand that had fed him for almost half a century.

"Thank you very much, Mr. Stengel," intoned Kefauver. "We appreciate your presence here."

"Mr. Mickey Mantle," said Senator Kefauver. "Will you come around?"

Mantle, wearing a new suit, a striped tie, and a sheepish expression on his face, walked to the table. His crew cut was neatly brushed, and his manner was relaxed. Stengel had done enough to relieve any tensions that may have been in the room at the outset.

"Mr. Mantle," Kefauver began in a serious tone, "do you have any observations with reference to the applicability of antitrust laws to baseball?"

A small grin escaped from the edges of Mickey's mouth. He leaned forward slowly and spoke clearly into the microphone.

"My views," said the country boy from Oklahoma, "are just about the same as Casey's."

Now the hearing room exploded with laughter. Stengel sat back in his chair and winked at Edna. She squeezed Mary Lavagetto's hand.

"I think," said Kefauver with a wry smile on his face, "this would be an appropriate time to adjourn."

That evening on television's Huntley-Brinkley report of the day's newsworthy events, nearly two minutes of film were devoted to the event. With the film running under the credits at the end of the program, David Brinkley was laughing almost uncontrollably. Casey Stengel had clearly become a television star. Several weeks after his performance, he was still giving long-winded imitations of Kefauver's drawl for writers around the club.

Mantle spent a good part of the next day entertaining teammates with anecdotes of Stengel's performance. Mickey's one line speech before the committee was probably as well remembered in some circles as President Abraham Lincoln's two-minute oration at Gettysburg in 1863.

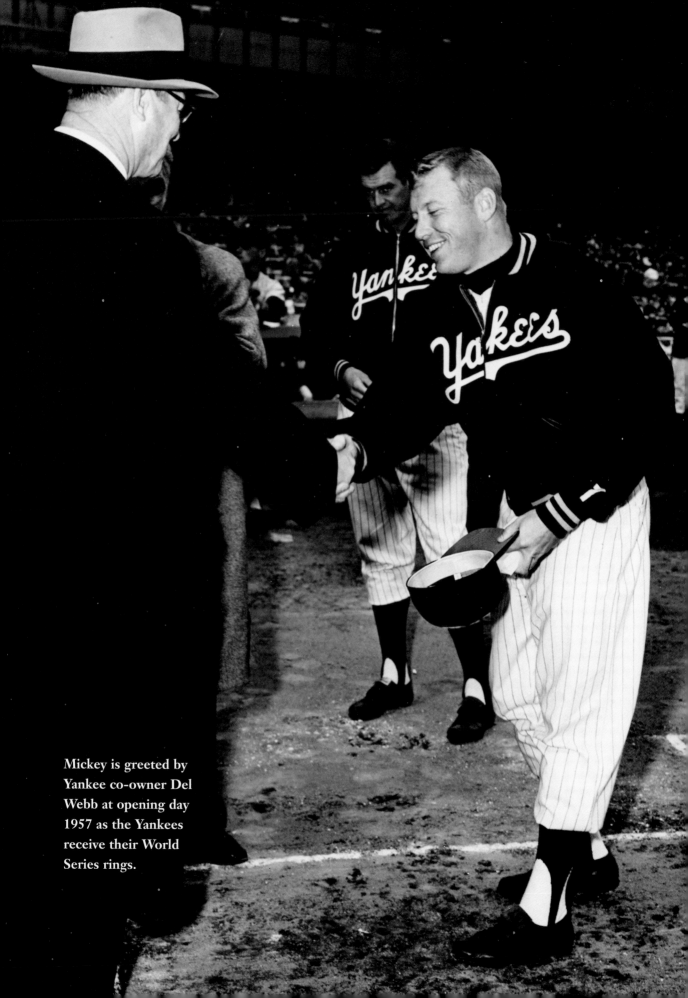

Mickey is greeted by Yankee co-owner Del Webb at opening day 1957 as the Yankees receive their World Series rings.

◆ ◆ ◆

An incredible thing happened in New York baseball in 1958. There was less of it than at any time since the professional game was invented. The Brooklyn Dodgers, who had so identified with and been identified by the borough of Brooklyn, moved to Los Angeles. The New York Giants, once the most celebrated and powerful team in the game, meekly followed suit, moving west to San Francisco.

Walter O'Malley, a corporate lawyer who had hustled his way into the Brooklyn hierarchy over a dozen years, got a sweetheart deal in Los Angeles on a place called Chavez Ravine. He was given use of the Los Angeles Coliseum, which seated 103,000 people, for his baseball team while he privately built Dodger Stadium on the gifted land.

Meanwhile, the Giants played in Seals Stadium in San Francisco and then leased a new field called Candlestick Park.

Their owner was Horace Stoneham, a heavy drinking Irishman who visited the site of his new park only once. He was there at noon on a bright, sunny day. He enjoyed the site. Then he left, approving the deal.

What Stoneham had missed was the fact that the winds of San Francisco, coming off the bay at that point, begin at about three in the afternoon and roar most of the rest of the day and into the evening.

"What I hate most about the place," Willie Mays once told me, "is that the peanut shells keep blowing in your eyes when you try and hit."

A small pitcher named Stu Miller was blown off the mound by San Francisco winds during the All-Star game of 1961.

While the Dodgers moved to Los Angeles and the Giants moved to San Francisco, the Yankees, under Stengel, moved to their ninth pennant in ten years.

In Stengel's first two seasons as the Yankee manager, the club had drawn over two million home fans at Yankee Stadium. By 1957, the last year in which there were three teams in New York, the Yankees slipped to a home attendance of 1,497,134.

The Yankee offices were incredibly optimistic that winter, sure that they would climb back in 1958 to the mark of two million in home attendance.

Owners Dan Topping, Del Webb, and especially general manager George Weiss just didn't get it. National League fans, sour at the loss of the Brooklyn Dodgers and New York Giants to "foreign cities" out West, simply stayed home.

The Yankees drew less in 1958 at home as the only big-league team in town than they had drawn in 1957 as the only team advertised to be staying in New York. The 1958 home attendance figure was 1,428,438—an embarrassingly small total.

Don Larsen, whose perfect game highlighted the '56 World Series, and Mantle, whose consistent play highlighted the '56 season, display their respective awards during a 1957 ceremony at Yankee Stadium.

Brooklyn fans were too emotionally locked into their former team to care for the Yankees. Giant fans, losing interest because of the team's failures since 1954, hardly seemed to care.

The Yankees, successful as they were, filled with glamorous players led by Mantle, Ford, and Berra, and arrogant about their control of baseball in New York, were beginning to get the cold shoulder.

Their own wealthy fans, those who came from Westchester, New Jersey, Connecticut, and posh Manhattan neighborhoods, were showing signs of boredom.

So the Yankees won. So they had Mantle. So they played in the World Series every year. So they had the most successful manager in the history of the game.

So what.

It was a case of too much too often.

The Yankees, winning so frequently, so convincingly, and with such ease, had lost the drama of victory for the public.

As Stengel passed his sixty-eighth birthday on July 30, 1958, press speculation began about his possible successors. Nobody would take Stengel on face-to-face on the subject, but sportswriters for local newspapers kidded about it among themselves, wrote about it with unnamed sources, and speculated about it in magazine articles.

Milwaukee won the National League pennant again in 1958. The Yankees lost the first two games at home, rallied behind Don Larsen, who had pitched the 1956 perfect game in the Series, for a win the third game. They fell behind three games to one in the 1958 Series when Warren Spahn beat Whitey Ford in a battle of future Hall of Famers.

There was an air of boredom throughout the entire Series. Somehow, it was saved, especially for New York fans, when the Yankees rallied to win the last three games and take the Series in seven games.

Mantle played all seven games and hit two home runs, one off Lew Burdette, who had embarrassed him the year before.

In 1959 the Yankees never did get going. Mantle had a poor year, for him, with only 31 home runs, 75 runs batted in, and a .285 batting average.

Al Lopez, who led the Cleveland Indians to a record 111 wins in 1954, beating the Yankees out, won another pennant—this time with the Chicago White Sox. The Yankees finished third, their worst season ever under Stengel.

Now the heat really built in the press about Stengel's future. He was at an age when most managers are long gone. He was grouchy about his bad team. He seemed to enjoy talking more about his own past career as a player in New York than he did about the current Yankees he managed. He had a press who fawned over him, but he also had a few aggressive young sportswriters who were not so friendly.

Stories began to appear with regularity about how Stengel slept on the bench, how he turned authority over to his coaches, how he was crusty in front of the players during trips when his wife Edna was present. He even screamed at Mantle, Ford, and Berra when he thought they had let him down.

There was another factor at work that would impact on Stengel's future.

A young coach, Ralph Houk, who had been an insignificant backup catcher, was being looked on as a future Yankee manager. Houk had hit .272 in 91 big-league games with the Yankees over an eight-year period. He had then managed the farm club at Denver before rejoining the Yankees as a coach in 1958. By 1959, at the age of forty, he was generally considered to be the heir to the throne.

Houk had been a World War II hero, could hold his liquor, was a man's man, and never expressed a word of disloyalty about the organization. He was also a favorite of owner Dan Topping. And Houk knew how to ingratiate himself to the important players on the team, players like Mantle, with a kidding remark or a needed boost.

Stengel's days were clearly numbered.

Mantle, who was now approaching his twenty-eighth year at the end of the 1959 season, and was the father of three sons, no longer needed the surrogate father that Stengel had been for him.

Their romance was ending.

Mantle was about to enter a new stage in his baseball life. While midlife crisis outside of sports occurs as one's fortieth birthday approaches, it occurs much earlier for a ballplayer—at twenty-six, twenty-seven, twenty-eight, depending on how long the player has been in the game.

Mantle joined the Yankees while still only eighteen years old in 1950. With DiMaggio's retirement, he had not had to wait to become a regular in DiMaggio's old position in right field the following season. He had established himself as a star within a few years. He was the most important, the most famous player in the game by the time he was twenty-six years old.

Mantle's injuries, his sour moods, his intense self-evaluations had caused some damage to his positive image as a young star.

By 1959 there were as many fans booing him for his strikeouts at Yankee Stadium as there were cheering his numerous home runs. No matter what he did on the field, it never seemed to be enough for some people. After all, he was Mickey Mantle, the successor to Joe DiMaggio, the guy who would make fans forget Ruth, Gehrig, and the rest.

His career, as 1959 ended, was in danger of sliding downhill with unfulfilled expectations.

All that would change with a trade made on December 11, 1959.

On that date Kansas City sent first baseman Kent Hadley, infielder Joe DeMaestri, and outfielder Roger Maris to the Yankees. In return, Kansas City got Hank Bauer, Marv Throneberry, Don Larsen, and Norm Siebern.

That trade would change Mantle's life.

A few days earlier, Yankee owner Dan Topping had been cornered in a New York restaurant. He was asked about Stengel's future.

"The managerial situation will be examined," he said.

The coming of Maris to New York and the going of Stengel, less than a year away, would impact heavily on the future of Mickey Mantle.

Detroit's Al Kaline was generally considered Mantle's chief American League rival for best player. Here they are during the height of their careers in 1959.

Dynamic Duo

T here was an air of tension around the Yankees spring training camp in 1960 that had never been felt before.

The Yankees hadn't won in 1959. That was enough to make owners Del Webb and Dan Topping grumpy, enough to make Casey Stengel even grumpier, and more than enough to make sour George Weiss unbearable.

Weiss had cut Mickey Mantle's salary again—to $62,000 a year after a long holdout. At the age of twenty-eight, when he should have been approaching his peak years as a player and breadwinner, he was moving downwards.

Stengel wasn't much help. After almost fifty years in the game, Casey understood every message, every nuance, every sign of change. He could clearly see that this was to be his last season—probably win or lose. Ralph Houk was ready to manage. Owner Dan Topping, who admired Houk's war record as a ranger as much as he admired his baseball acumen, was ready to give him the job, regardless of the Yankees' record.

Mantle had batted only .285 with 31 homers and 75 RBI. The only department in which he led the league was in strikeouts. He was approaching his tenth season in Yankee pinstripes. That was more than twice as long as the average big-league player could expect. He was so far above average that these figures were meaningless for him.

Still, his legs were getting worse, his shoulder ached, his knees were frequently sore, his back bothered him, and to make matters worse, he suffered from self-inflicted hangovers.

This was clearly the crisis season of Mantle's career. He responded like a trooper.

The appearance of his new teammate, Roger Maris, changed Mantle's status. Mantle was now the slugging leader of a team preparing for a comeback. As good as Yogi Berra was, he was clearly slipping fast. Elston Howard, Moose Skowron, John Blanchard, and Bob Cerv were all useful power hitters.

But Maris was something else.

Maris was made for Yankee Stadium. He had an incredibly quick bat, a line drive swing, and a level of concentration that Mantle had never seen before.

Maris played the game with a single purpose. He wanted to get rich. He was not there because he loved baseball. Actually, as a kid and as a young professional adult, football was his favorite sport. He was twenty-five years old when he joined the Yankees—a quiet, intense, humorless slugger who had grown up in the bitterly cold climate of Fargo, North Dakota.

"I remember when he flew up from spring training that first year and I picked him up at the airport," said Julie Isaacson, a local labor leader and Yankee fan who had befriended Maris. "He was wearing white socks, white buckskin shoes, a polo shirt and a bright sports jacket. 'For crissakes, Roger,' I told him, 'get a suit. This is New York.' He didn't care about appearances. All he cared about was hitting the ball, being with his family and getting wealthy."

A subtle change was taking place in the minds of the fans as Maris exploded on the scene in the 1960 season. He was considered an outsider, an interloper, a stranger in the midst of these familiar Yankees—Yogi, Whitey Ford, Moose Skowron, and especially, Mantle.

This was Mickey's team, not Roger's. Fans wanted Mickey to know that by their cheers. If he struck out now, they accepted it. They knew a home run would soon follow.

If Roger struck out, they booed him. After all, he was the outsider. He had been brought in to guarantee a pennant for 1960 and another Series win. He was not allowed to fail.

Maris hit two home runs on opening day of the 1960 season and moved on to a wonderful season with 39 homers, 112 RBI, and the MVP title.

Family Day, 1959. Mickey, Merlyn, Billy and Mickey Jr. with Whitey Ford and his wife (Joan) and their children.

Mickey won the home run title with 40. He had 94 RBI and a .275 average.

The relationship between Maris and Mantle was strained at first, but improved with time—in part because of the efforts of Julie Isaacson. The labor leader and Yankee friend had gotten Mantle and Maris together with outfielder Bob Cerv in a Queens apartment about thirty minutes from the Stadium.

As they got to know each other, away from the game and its stresses, each saw that the other was interested in helping the team win. They came to accept each other's widely divergent personalities.

Mantle liked to laugh, was a hard drinker, and was quick to enjoy the city's nightlife.

Maris was quiet, often sullen, independent, not a leader of men, but also never jealous of Mantle's fame and recognition. Maris was one of the few baseball players who might have enjoyed playing the game in an empty stadium, with neither fans nor press around—if the price was right.

Mantle, though he rarely showed it publicly, bathed in the applause after a big home run. He enjoyed the adulation.

Roger's father was always around to share his success. Mantle sorely missed his father, dead when he was just beginning his climb to fame.

While Mickey drank heavily and was chased by adoring women in the Yankee hotels on the road, Maris was rarely to be found in the hotel bar. More often, he would spend his off time in his hotel room, watching television. He might go to a quiet restaurant with a friend or to a local pool hall where he liked to play billiards.

In 1960, in his first MVP year as a Yankee, he was still not a well-recognized face.

As the Yankees won the pennant again, Stengel's tenth in his twelve seasons as skipper, rumors swirled around the club that this would be his last year on the job.

He had turned seventy in July, and while Casey tried to keep it quiet, Edna threw a big party for him in their Essex House suite in Manhattan, where he lived during the season.

Ralph Houk, ambitious about the job, let it be known that the Detroit Tigers were very interested in gaining his services as a manager. Something would have to happen by the end of the year. Something did.

Before all that, the Yankees played the Pirates in a stirring seven-game World Series—one of the strangest in baseball history.

The Yankees won three games by the scores of 16-3, 10-0, and 12-0. They lost games by the scores of 6-4, 3-2, and 5-2.

As the seventh game in Pittsburgh approached, Stengel was taking a beating in the press for starting right-hander Art Ditmar instead of Whitey Ford in the opener.

Stengel felt a right-handed Pittsburgh lineup, led by Roberto Clemente, Gino Cimoli, Don Hoak, Bill Mazeroski, and Dick Groat, would be slowed by Ditmar, a right-hander who had won fifteen games in that 1960 season. Stengel wanted to save his ace, Whitey Ford, for the Yankee Stadium games.

"I thought my right-hander would make them hit grounders," Stengel said later. "I didn't know all the grounders would bounce into the outfield."

The seventh game of the Series was one of the most thrilling ever played—and probably one of the best remembered.

Bill Mazeroski broke it up with a home run in the bottom of the

**Cardinals great Stan Musial and Mickey Mantle never played against each
other, except in All Star games, such as this one in 1960.**

ninth inning of a 9-9 game off right-hander Ralph Terry. Mazeroski would
become famous for that one blow, and Terry would become infamous for
the homer. (Terry gained a measure of revenge two years later when he
beat the San Francisco Giants 1-0 in the seventh game.) Willie McCovey
lined to second baseman Bobby Richardson for the final out of the 1960
World Series.

There was one play in the seventh game in that Series that, for
Mantle and many Yankees, overshadowed the loss.

In the eighth inning Bill Virdon, later to manage the Yankees, hit a
sharp ground ball to shortstop Tony Kubek. The ball hit a pebble in front
of Kubek, bounced up at a strange angle, and smashed into his throat.

Kubek was forced out of the game.

After Mazeroski homered over left fielder Yogi Berra's head for the
Pittsburgh triumph, the press crowded into the tiny visitors' clubhouse at
Forbes Field.

Kubek was lying down on a small training table with a towel over his

Mickey makes some kid's day.

throat. Yankee trainer, Gus Mauch, had done what he could to stop the flow of blood. A doctor was needed, and the Pittsburgh team physician had been delayed in getting through the stands and into the Yankee clubhouse.

Mantle, hoping to escape the press, walked into the training room. He saw the bloody towel Kubek held up to his throat. He immediately burst into tears.

Kubek and Mantle were not particularly close. Kubek was a religious youngster from Milwaukee whose drink of choice was malted milk. Still, he was a wonderful player for the Yankees, with enormous pride in the team. He could play the outfield as well as he played the infield. From his rookie year in 1957, Kubek was admired by Mantle, who respected his intelligence. Kubek, in turn, respected Mantle's enormous skills and the intensity with which he played.

For the most part, Mantle had played with incredible devotion to the

Yankees. There was something mystical to players about wearing that uniform. Once a player came to the team, as Maris did that season, and as Kubek had done a few years earlier, he was, in Shakespeare's words, "grappled to their soul with hoops of steel."

The injury to Kubek was as forceful an emotional experience as the illness of any family member.

Mantle reminisced after his 1968 retirement about the 1960 defeat by Pittsburgh. "That was the most bitter loss of my career," he said. "It hurt so much because we all knew that we were a better team than Pittsburgh was. We were supposed to win that thing. We showed it clearly in those games in which we pounded them. We scored nine runs in the seventh game of the World Series. How could anybody believe, with that many runs, we wouldn't win."

On October 15, the Yankees called a press conference at the swank Savoy Hilton Hotel in Manhattan to announce their plans regarding manager Casey Stengel.

Dan Topping, who made very few appearances before the sporting press, read a statement. The room was filled with angry reporters who had been told several different versions of Stengel's future and were clearly fed up. They wanted this situation resolved so they could end their baseball coverage for the year and move on to more important things—like preparing for the annual Baseball Writers dinner and show at the Waldorf-Astoria Hotel.

Topping read a prepared statement. It was a little confusing. It stated clearly that Stengel would not be back in 1961, but it made mention of future payments to him. It seemed that Stengel was being forcibly retired, but paid well for his pain.

Now Stengel moved to the microphones. That was the biggest mistake the Yankees made that day. They should have announced Casey's situation long after he had left town.

Casey wore a new blue suit. His hair was plastered down. It glowed a bit in the television lights. His shoes were highly polished. He looked like a 70-year-old altar boy.

"I'll never make the mistake of being seventy again," he said.

"Casey, were you fired?" a reporter shouted from the crowd.

"No, I wasn't fired," he bellowed. "I was paid up in full."

"The Associated Press has a bulletin, Casey. It says you were fired. What about it?" yelled another reporter.

"What do I care what the AP says. Their opinion ain't going to send me into any fainting spell. Anyway, what about the UP?"

After the laughter stopped, Stengel continued.

"Mr. Webb and Mr. Topping have started a program for the Yankees. They needed a solution as to when to discharge a man on account of age. My services are no longer required by this club and I told them if that was their idea not to worry about me."

"Were you fired?" a reporter bellowed, trying hard to get Casey to use that term.

"Quit, fired, quit, discharged, use whatever you damn please," Casey said. "I don't care. You don't see me crying do you about it?"

"What will you do now?"

"Have another drink," said Stengel. "That's what."

Forced retirement is probably the best description of the events of that day.

A month later George Weiss would also be quietly "discharged," as the Yankees cleaned out the old and brought in younger men.

Weiss would soon be hired by the new expansion team in New York, the New York Mets. He would convince his old pal Stengel to manage that team for him in the first season of 1962.

Stengel stayed with the Mets until a fall and a broken hip ended his active managerial career in 1965. After that, he remained a consultant to the team and was listed as a vice president until his death in 1975. He was elected to Baseball's Hall of Fame in 1966. A street outside of Shea Stadium, where the New York Mets have played since 1964, is named Casey Stengel Plaza.

Mickey Mantle said he was upset when the Yankees released Stengel.

"Sure he was getting old and fell asleep on the bench once in a while," he told me years later, "but he was so successful for the club. They could have done something special for him, just the way the Mets did after he left them. I'll always love him. He did an awful lot for me."

Mantle spent a good part of that winter of 1960–61 thinking about the new operation of the team.

Lee MacPhail, the farm director, was promoted to general manager after Weiss left, and Ralph Houk, as expected, was named manager of the Yankees.

Mantle would now be playing for a former teammate, someone he had been associated with ever since he joined the team in 1951.

Ralph Houk was a burly man with a temper kept under control—most of the time. He talked in choppy phrases. He never offered much in the way of public opinions and could stare down a sportswriter when he didn't like a question. Always, always, he protected the players. As far as Houk was concerned, no player ever made an error. It was always the official scorer, the umpire, or the fans who caused a man to drop a fly ball, to miss a grounder, to blow a line drive.

It ingratiated his players to him to such a degree that many of the Yankees, and later the Tigers and Red Sox teams who played for him, overachieved. They never wanted to be seen as weak in the eyes of the man who so represented masculine strength to them.

Houk's first words to every player joining the team were always the same. He would point to a cluster of sportswriters standing in the corner of the Yankee clubhouse and whisper, "Never tell those guys nothin'."

As his eleventh season with the Yankees approached, Mantle could almost feel the changes around the team. It was not just having a new general manager and manager. There were new players, many of whom were a little afraid of him. There were new executives around the club and new faces among the sportswriters. And it was unsettling to find an ever increasing number of television reporters and cameras.

More and more often Mantle spent his pregame time in the trainer's room, taping his legs, exchanging gossip with other players, resting after long nights, and staying away from reporters.

He often skipped batting practice in the early 1960s, a major disappointment for fans who came to the park early to experience the thrill of a Mantle home run clearing a distant fence.

Maris, still painfully shy in public, worked quietly in spring training on improving his line drive Stadium swing.

Shortly after he reported, Mantle was summoned to Ralph Houk's office.

"Mick, I want you to be the leader on this team. We have a lot of young players. I want you to show them the way," Houk said.

"What do I do?" asked Mantle.

"Just lead by example. Play hard and be yourself," Houk said.

Unofficially, Mantle had become the leader of the team. There was no title of captain. The Yankees had refused to do that ever since the death of Lou Gehrig in 1941. He was the one and only Yankee captain. Gehrig continued to hold that honorary position during all the years that Mantle played, though in later years Thurman Munson and Don Mattingly would be named Yankee captains.

The 1961 season would be one of the most thrilling in Yankee baseball history.

The "M and M" boys were about to electrify the country. MVP Roger Maris started slowly in 1961. He did not hit one home run through the first 10 games on the Yankees schedule. He finally homered in Detroit off Paul Foytack. He would go six more games before he hit another home run—this one off Petro Ramos of the Minnesota Twins.

By June 11, he had 20 homers. By July 2, he had 30 homers. By July 25, he had 40 homers.

That was just about the time Baseball Commissioner Ford Frick, an old newsman and friend of Babe Ruth's, decided to address the question many fans had been asking.

Maris and Mantle were hitting home runs that summer at a pace that could equal or pass the 1927 home run pace of Ruth. The Babe had hit 60 homers in a 154-game season in 1927. But Maris and Mantle were playing in the new, expanded 162-game season in 1961.

Frick determined that any home run record would have to have a special notation attached to it, later defined as an asterisk. He made no mention of other records—pitching records, games played, ERAs, or stolen bases. It was only the sacred record of the Babe that Frick, his pal, was working to salvage.

As the press attacked this idea of a special mark, this asterisk, Mantle and Maris continued to homer at a record rate.

The more home runs Maris hit, the more he was booed.

The more home runs Mantle hit, the more he was cheered.

Maris reacted to the increase in tension with more than his usual surliness and by disassociating himself, as much as was possible, from the glare of publicity.

Mantle, behind in the race most of the year, reacted with humor amd with a rare show of public wit. He was taking the race more lightly.

When Mantle hit his 48th homer of the season, on August 31, he shouted to Roger, "I got my guy, Raj, you get yours."

He was referring to the fact that Lou Gehrig hit 47 homers in that 1927 season when Ruth hit 60. Mantle was now behind Maris and was playing Gehrig to Roger's Ruth. Maris had 51 homers that last day of August.

Newspapers referred to them as the "M and M" boys in their challenge to the Ruth-Gehrig total home run mark.

No matter what the Yankees did as a team or what other Yankees did individually in any game, the press wrote mostly about the "M and M" boys.

"It got so that I felt badly for the rest of our guys," Mantle said later. "Somebody would win a game with a homer, or Whitey would pitch a shutout, and the reporters would crowd around Roger and me."

Old Yankee fans, motivated by memories of Ruth, attacked Roger verbally at each game. As his home run numbers grew, dislike for him increased as well. He was threatening the status of an idol. Through no

A pitcher's nightmare, Mickey Mantle followed by Roger Maris. In 1961 they hit a combined 115 home runs.

fault of his own, simply because of his remarkable talent, he threatened to diminish the glory of Ruth in the eyes of rabid Ruth fans.

Mantle, on the other hand, was the anchor of Yankee legend. The torch had been passed from Ruth to Gehrig to DiMaggio to Mantle. If there was to be a challenger to the Babe's record, fans were only willing for Mantle to be the one.

Mickey had taken a preliminary run at the record in his Triple Crown year, 1956, when he hit 52 homers.

As the Yankees moved into September, an enormous amount of attention was focused on the race. Newspapers from all over the country sent reporters to cover the Yankees. Radio stations had interviewers around them constantly. Television did standups from the clubhouse after every game, sometimes waiting for two or three hours while the two players lounged in the training room or took saunas in a bathtub.

"I felt badly for Roger," Mantle said many years later. "He just wanted to play baseball. He didn't want to talk to the press about it."

By September forty or fifty reporters, radio interviewers, and camera people surrounded Maris after each game. He would stand against his locker, his arm on a metal rail, his eyes fixed straight ahead. He would answer all the questions in a laconic manner, biting off the words as if each statement was a very painful exercise.

On days he had failed to homer, it might be a little quicker interview, but still, he was there.

Mantle, who had learned after eleven years how to evade the press, was rarely available on days when he failed to hit a home run. He would josh with sportswriters when he did hit one. Mostly he kidded about Roger's pursuit of the Babe, now that September had come and his own chances were slipping away.

That summer of 1961 was the year that Mantle crossed over from being a great baseball player into a figure of immeasurable love, admiration, and esteem.

Maris had taken on the unpleasant role of villain. He was the man who was challenging the beloved Babe. Mantle was the hero of this epic— no matter what transpired.

Mail poured into the Yankee clubhouse for both players. Most of Mickey's mail was warm, supportive, friendly, and encouraging. The mail for Maris was often hate filled, angry, or threatening. He was called names, derided for his joyless demeanor, and charged with being a flash in the pan. One of the most derisive names for a big-league ballplayer, "busher," was often thrown at him. A busher is a big-league ballplayer that fans, the press or even his teammates believe is not of big-league caliber, but rather belongs in the minors or bush leagues.

The situation was outrageous. Roger Maris was, simply, a wonderful baseball player who never recognized his obligation to the fans. They hated him for that, and for even getting close to the famed Ruth record.

Mantle had never been anything but a Yankee, and many fans identified with him. By 1961, as he approached the age of thirty, he had been a Stadium hero for over a decade. To many observers, it felt like a good part of their lives had been spent with Mickey.

The month of September was as thrilling a time in baseball as the game has ever seen.

Maris hit his 56th homer on September 9. Mantle had his 53rd the next day.

Mantle was suffering from a head cold as the race continued. On the Yankees charter flight back from Boston, broadcaster Mel Allen approached him.

"I have a doctor who will fix you up," Allen offered.

Mel Allen had been around the Yankees since 1939. He had witnessed Gehrig's retirement speech on July 4, 1939, the 56-game hitting streak of Joe DiMaggio, all the excitement of the championship years, and the growth of Mantle as the present team's most heroic star.

Allen had never married. His life revolved around the Yankees and these players. Mantle agreed to take Allen's suggestion and visit the doctor who could fix him up.

The doctor Allen sent Mantle to was later nicknamed Dr. Feelgood, and his drug of choice, unknown to Mantle or to Allen, was amphetamines. President Kennedy had gone to this doctor, too. He came highly recommended. Dr. Max Jacobson injected Mantle with his magic potion in the buttocks. By the next day an infection had set in, and Mantle was confined to his bed.

He was forced into a stay at Lenox Hill Hospital. He was there on October 1, 1961, when Maris hit his 61st homer of the season to break Ruth's record of 60.

"A season's a season," Maris said when questioned about the validity of the record in light of Frick's slanted ruling.

"I watched that game on television," Mantle told me later. "When he hit it, I just cried. I wanted to be there. I wanted to challenge the mark myself, and I knew how Roger felt."

The line drive home run off Boston right-hander Tracy Stallard had gone about 365 feet into the right-field stands.

The 1961 Yankees, led by (from left) Roger Maris, Yogi Berra, Mickey Mantle, and Moose Skowron, set a record for home runs in a season (240) that stood for 35 years.

While Mantle sat in his hospital bed, teammates Moose Skowron, John Blanchard, and Hector Lopez pushed Maris out on the field again after he had reached the Yankee dugout.

He had a small, tight grin on his face. His deep-set eyes looked tired. His crew cut was cut close to the scalp. He held his baseball cap in his hand, uncomfortably looking this way and that, finally raising his cap toward the crowd in the stands.

"I don't think Roger ever got the credit for what he did," Mantle said many years later. "As far as I was concerned, that was the single greatest performance in baseball history. That season was the toughest one anyone ever went through."

Mantle recognized that in chasing the immortal Babe's record, he and Roger had faced enormous tensions, tensions which literally divided the country between those who wanted them to break the mark and those who wanted to see the Babe's record protected.

"What saddened me," said Clete Boyer, the Yankees third baseman that year and a very close friend of Roger's, "was that the Frick fuss took all the joy out of it for Roger. Sure, Roger hit 61 homers but to a lot of people, mostly because of Frick, it was a tainted record."

Boyer said that Roger never really verbalized his pain, but he could see it in his eyes for years afterwards.

"It was almost as if the drama ended when he stopped at 59 homers after game 154. It was like hitting a home run in an exhibition," said Boyer.

Ruth had hit his 60 home runs in 1927. That mark lasted for thirty-four years until Roger's amazing feat of 61 home runs in 1961. By 1996 Maris's record was in its thirty-fifth year.

Maris may have had his record, but still he received little public affection.

Mantle, who had failed to reach the record, came out of the 1961 season as the most beloved athlete in America.

Mantle and Maris, linked in baseball history by that extraordinary season, became close friends. They spent the next five seasons together before Maris was traded to the St. Louis Cardinals on December 8, 1966, for journeyman infielder Charlie Smith.

Maris played for St. Louis in 1967 and 1968, was on two pennant-winning teams, and retired after the 1968 World Series. He was thirty-four years old.

He was given a beer distributorship in Gainesville, Florida, by St. Louis Cardinals' owner August A. "Gussie" Busch. The beer baron who owned the team appreciated Maris's efforts on behalf of his team.

Maris worked that business until he became ill late in 1983. He attended ceremonies at Yankee Stadium on July 21, 1984, at which time his uniform number nine was retired. A plaque was placed in the Yankees monument park for him. It read:

Roger Eugene Maris
against all odds in 1961 he became the only player to hit more
than 60 home runs in a single season
in belated recognition of one of baseball's greatest achievements ever
his 61 in '61.

Early in 1985, I visited with Maris in his offices at the Maris Distributing Company building in Gainesville.

He made a little joke as we shook hands. "I just spoke to Shannon [Mike Shannon had been a teammate and friend with the St. Louis Cardinals] and he said you only want to see me now in case I die before the twenty-fifth anniversary of the home run year next season."

"It's the twenty-fifth anniversary of your 1960 arrival in New York as a Yankee," I said.

Maris smiled. He didn't believe that explanation either.

About twenty minutes into our conversation, the phone rang. It was Mickey Mantle calling from his home in Dallas. He told Roger he was going to be in Florida for a few days. They made a golf date. They talked a few more minutes, with Roger laughing at some of Mickey's stories—all sprinkled liberally with obscenities. He asked to speak to me by identifying me with a two-word curse.

"Don't you go ripping Roger," Mantle admonished me. "I'll come up there and kick your ass."

I told him only young reporters do that to young players—and none of us were young anymore. Mantle laughed heartily. Then he hung up.

"He's been calling almost every day," Maris said.

Maris began talking about Mantle in an unemotional and straight-forward manner. .

"It didn't matter what I did, or how many home runs I hit," Maris said. "Mickey Mantle was always the New York Yankees."

On Saturday, December 14, 1985, Roger Maris died of cancer at the M. D. Anderson Hospital and Tumor Institute in Houston. He was fifty-one years old.

Mantle received a call from Whitey Ford about Roger's death. He wept into the phone. Later he was interviewed at home. "You always knew he was your friend," he said. "He was the kind of guy who would tell you so, just to make you feel better. Not enough people got to know him that way—that's all. What a great guy."

Mantle flew to Florida where he was committed to a golf appearance. Then he teamed up with Whitey Ford, flying to Fargo, North Dakota, Roger's boyhood home, where he was to be buried.

The funeral for Maris was held in Fargo on December 17 at Saint Mary's Church. Dozens of former teammates attended, with Mantle and Ford in a front row.

Mantle had arrived earlier that same day. Coming directly from the tropical climate of Florida, he was wearing the lightweight tan slacks, polo shirt, white socks, and loafers he had worn down South. He carried a lightweight windbreaker over his arm. When he walked out of the Fargo airport, a huge thermometer registered the temperature: 17 degrees below zero.

Bishop James S. Sullivan conducted the service. When he was finished, he asked members of the audience to say a few words about Roger. Hometown people stood up to speak. Old friends reminisced. Family members remembered many of Roger's adventures. Mantle sat in the church, his head down and tears in his eyes. He did not speak.

Finally, Clete Boyer, probably of all the Yankees the closest to Roger, addressed the crowd. He told some funny stories about Roger's appetite. Mantle smiled at the memories.

"That was the most nervous I had been in my life," said Boyer. There were twelve pallbearers escorting Roger's casket into St. Mary 's church that afternoon. There were five old hometown friends of Roger's and seven former players—Ford, Shannon, Skowron, Boyer, Herzog, Allison, and Mantle.

Bobby Richardson, former teammate, friend, and religious leader of the Yankees, delivered the eulogy for Maris. He spoke of Roger's baseball skills and his humility. He told a story about how he had been visited one year by Roger at his South Carolina home. Bobby's son was in an American Legion game that day, and a line drive had gotten past him.

"He's been watching me too much," Maris said, with his usual self-deprecating modesty.

Richardson's eulogy ended with his comments that many of Roger's problems in New York started with the press. "That might keep Roger from the Hall of Fame. Roger is in God's Hall of Fame. In life, the honors are soon forgotten. God's Hall of Fame is for eternity," Richardson said.

After the funeral service was over, Mantle walked up to Bobby Richardson and told him how touched he was by the eulogy.

"I don't like funerals. I never go," Mantle told Richardson. "The last one I went to was my father's, in 1952. This was really nice. I want you to do mine," he said.

Neither of them could have imagined that less than ten years later, Richardson would be in Lover's Lane Church in Dallas, delivering a eulogy for Mantle.

Mickey was a
star off the
field as well.

Basking

R oger *Maris took a terrible beating from the press in the spring of 1962.*

The Yankees had moved from their training site on Florida's west coast at St. Petersburg to a new complex on the east coast at Fort Lauderdale.

Each day the same events would occur. One reporter or another would get into a battle with Maris. Instead of shining in the glory of the 61 homers in 1961, he was thrust into controversy. He was attacked in the press by sports columnists Jimmy Cannon, Milton Gross, and Dan Parker. He was belittled by Hall of Famer Rogers Hornsby, a New York Mets coach that spring, for not hitting his 61 homers in 154 games— and for doing it with a modest average of .269 instead of coming close to Babe Ruth's mark of .365 for his 1927 record.

As spring training continued, Maris's tension increased, and he became more abrasive, less willing to

talk to anyone around the ballpark. This attitude included reporters, fans, and even Yankee teammates. He withdrew into himself and seemed to regret that the previous year had ever catapulted him into the public personality he had become.

While all this was going on, Mickey Mantle was sailing smoothly through spring training. He was very much at ease out of the spotlight. (Roger unhappily had replaced him for the first time in his Yankee career.) Mantle was gaining more respect daily as a veteran Yankee player, an old-timer, and perhaps, for the first time, as a legend with stature equal to Ruth, Gehrig, and DiMaggio.

"That was the year the pressure really eased on me," Mantle once told me. "There was so much pressure on Roger, so much fuss after the homers, that I could just concentrate on playing ball. Why, there were even days when not a single sportswriter asked me for an interview."

Both Maris and Mantle were doing well in the early days of the 1962 season. It was soon evident, however, that although this would be a good year for both, it would be nothing like 1961.

Maris wound up with 33 homers that season, batted .256, and had 100 RBI.

Mantle, who missed over a month of action with a severely pulled hamstring muscle, batted .321 in 123 games, knocked in 89 runs, and hit 30 homers.

It earned him his third most valuable player title. Maris had won the title the two previous years.

There were several players who changed the climate around the Yankees that year. Youngsters Joe Pepitone, Tom Tresh, Jim Bouton, and Phil Linz were altering the attitude in the clubhouse.

While games were still taken seriously, the clubhouse atmosphere was different. These young players recognized the futility of agonizing over a score that couldn't be changed, and win or lose, they had a good time in the clubhouse after games.

It was less raucous after a loss, to be sure, but the hanging of heads, the morose staring at the lockers, and the stark silence in the clubhouse that had formerly accompanied a Yankee loss were gone.

After a victory there was the loud laughter of overgrown children, which most of them were. They slapped each other on bare backs and buttocks with towels from the shower, played pranks on the more gullible, and as a joke, continually stole private property from each other.

After winning games, Mantle and Ford—now the veterans of the team along with Yogi Berra—would often join in.

After losses, they stayed aloof but could not control their laughter when Linz, Bouton, or Pepitone did or said something particularly outrageous.

This season, Mantle's twelfth as a Yankee, he could see the end coming, despite another strong year. His body was beginning to betray him more severely.

Veteran players get hurt more than young players, to be sure. They also heal more slowly, a cruel reality for the aging athlete.

"Mickey was always great to me," said Joe Pepitone, the wildly rowdy kid from Brooklyn. "He would take me out to dinner and he would always pay. He helped me on the field. He would laugh at some of our silliness. I may not have used my talent as well as I should have, but Mick never got on me. I think he always liked me. I know he always laughed at me. Besides, he was just another guy to me. Joe DiMaggio was my hero."

The Yankees won their third pennant in a row in 1962, their second under Ralph Houk's managing, and headed for a World Series against the San Francisco Giants.

The Giants had edged out the Dodgers in a playoff again, as they had in 1951 with the Bobby Thomson homer off Ralph Branca.

When the playoff game was over and the Dodgers were defeated, their locker room was closed to the press. Only one player came out to be interviewed—veteran outfielder Duke Snider.

"When Thomson hit the homer in 1951 and we got beat I told my wife, 'At least I won't ever have to go through *this* again.' What am I going to tell her now?"

Willie Mays and Mickey Mantle, friendly rivals from a decade earlier in New York, would meet for the second time in a World Series.

Neither did very much in the Series, as is disappointingly often the case in baseball with big stars. Mantle batted .120 and Mays batted .250. Neither hit a home run.

The Series ended when future Hall of Famer Willie McCovey lined a bullet toward right in the bottom of the ninth inning of a 1-0 seventh game. Yankee second baseman Bobby Richardson caught the ball at eye level as the tying run and the lead run for the Giants were on base. Ralph Terry, who had given up that famous Pittsburgh home run to Bill Mazeroski, now had a 1-0 seventh-game World Series win.

Mantle, who had played in only 123 games that season but had won the most valuable player crown anyway, found himself the subject of discussion in the press. There was speculation that he had not truly earned the award in 1962 but was voted Most Valuable Player for previous seasons' performances when he had not been given the award.

All the talk actually helped Mickey in contract negotiations with the

Yankees. Under new general manager Lee MacPhail, Mantle was rewarded for the first time with a $100,000 a year contract, the ultimate salary prize in baseball.

No player had ever been paid more than that, even though Babe Ruth's $80,000 salary in 1930 was the equivalent of five times that amount.

Not until 1965, when Sandy Koufax and Don Drysdale held out in tandem, was the $100,000 salary level crossed. The Dodgers, knowing they would go nowhere without the two future Hall of Famers, gave in a few days before spring training ended. Koufax signed for $125,000, and Drysdale was paid $112,000. By 1996 salaries of seven and eight million dollars a year were not uncommon in big-league baseball.

Mantle never earned more than $100,000, but unlike many aging stars, his salary was never cut as his production decreased in the middle 1960s.

The 1963 season was a trying year for Mantle. He broke his foot when he crashed into an outfield wall in Baltimore while attempting a catch. He hit .314 in 65 games, with 15 homers.

On the plus side, he hit one of his favorite home runs that season. It was also my favorite Mantle home run.

The previous September 10, 1962, Mantle, batting right-handed, had crashed a low curve off left-hander Hank Aguirre into the upper deck at Tiger Stadium.

It was Mantle's 400th career home run.

At this point, the home runs were being recorded each day with great fanfare. At the age of thirty, Mantle still had the potential for 500—or perhaps even 600 homers—if he played long enough.

Number 413 was historic.

No fair ball had ever been hit out of Yankee Stadium since the park opened in 1923. Ruth couldn't do it. Neither could Gehrig. DiMaggio didn't do it.

There was a legend about Josh Gibson, though. The catcher and star of the old Negro Leagues, which played many games at the Stadium while the Yankees were on the road, once did it, if the legend is true. Gibson was a right-handed hitter, and the distance would be well over 700 feet at that point.

Not very likely, though some black historians insist it happened. White-owned newspapers of the day did not cover Negro League games, while black-owned papers tended to exaggerate any accomplishment.

Whether Gibson did or did not hit a ball out of Yankee Stadium, certainly big-league baseball record keepers did not recognize any such feat.

Mantle longed to be the first one. He often asked about the Gibson

Maris, Willie Mays, and Mickey Mantle were the most feared sluggers in the early sixties.

legend on days when he hit some huge drive. John Drebinger, a sports-writer for the *New York Times*, who had covered Ruth and Gehrig in their prime and was still around the Yankees into his nineties, reminded Mantle he had never seen it done.

"Do you think anybody can do it?" Mantle asked Drebinger one day.

"I'll believe it when I see it," Drebinger dryly told Mantle.

On May 22, 1963, he almost, almost saw it.

Mantle caught a high fastball thrown by a bald-headed Kansas City A's reliever named Bill Fischer for home run number 413 of his career.

The ball left the bat in a high arch, zooming toward the stands in right, continued to climb, and hit the facing of the third deck about two feet from the top. It was still on the rise when it hit the front at the very top part of the stands and caromed back onto the field toward second base.

Mantle jogged toward first base, stopping to stare at the flight of the ball. He stood still as it crashed against the facade, then continued jogging home with the huge home run.

After the game, I asked him about the blast.

"I think I got all of it," he laughed.

Then he was asked if that was the hardest home run he had ever hit. It was clearly the longest.

"It hit the facade. It had to be," he said. Only Mantle, with his Oklahoma drawl, had pronounced the famous outer facing of the third deck known as the facade as "fuh-card."

In the *New York Post* the next day, I described our conversation and quoted Mickey as saying it hit the "fuh-card."

Then I wrote, "When you can hit them as far as Mickey does it hardly matters how you pronounce them."

The Associated Press reprinted my Mantle quote and following line. I got clippings on it from all over the country. *Time* magazine put the item in their People section, and that became my most memorable and favorite Mantle homer.

Mantle loved it because it was his longest home run ever, and I loved it because it earned me a little extra attention.

Mantle broke his foot a couple of weeks later, went home to Commerce, stayed there until late July, and returned for the last two and a half months of the season.

On August 4 Mantle pinch-hit against the Baltimore Orioles. It was his first at-bat in nearly two months. He hit a home run off left-hander George Brunet, the 416th home run of his career. It may have been one of the most dramatic home runs of Mickey's career. Yankee fans, now totally enamored of Mantle and totally soured on Maris, cheered themselves silly.

Now each home run seemed filled with a great sense of drama. Since Mantle was injured so frequently, and so much was made of the weak condition of his legs by the press each day, the fans acted as if each homer might be his last. It was always a possibility. The press constantly kept that possibility in the mind of Mantle's fans as they continued to refer to his declining skills.

As 1963 began, Mantle was six years away from the end of his career.

While he was out of the lineup with one of his many injuries, the Yankees never announced when he might be back. They called each injury "day to day"—whether it was Mantle or any other team member.

After several weeks I wrote a column in the *New York Post* about

The 1962 Yankees, Mantle's last team to win a championship, are feted at a ceremony at New York's City Hall.

Mantle's absence. I kidded the Yankees about always describing every injury as day to day.

"There is no Mickey Mantle," I wrote in late July. "He's only a figment of everyone's imagination."

Mantle, who took kidding about his physical ailments with ill humor, reacted badly. One day after he was well enough to resume taking batting practice, I approached him. He was not happy to see me. "You piss me off just standing there," he said. It took a few more home runs late that season before he would forgive me.

By the middle of September, the leg had improved. Mantle was running well, playing every day, and hitting fairly normally.

Then came the 1963 World Series against the Los Angeles Dodgers. It was a nightmare for the Yankees.

The Dodgers had Koufax, Drysdale, and Johnny Podres as their starting pitchers. Koufax won two games, Drysdale and Podres won a game each. (Podres was always a Brooklyn hero for winning two games in the 1955 World Series.) Ron Perranoski had two-thirds of an inning of perfect relief.

Mantle tried to keep the Yankees in the Series in what turned out to be the fourth and final game. The Dodgers had already won the first three.

Mickey caught a high fastball in the seventh inning off Koufax in a 1-0 game for his 15th Series homer—the one that tied Babe Ruth's Series mark. Mickey never hit 60 homers in a season as Ruth did, or 61 as Maris did, but he caught and later passed the Babe in Series homers.

Over that winter Yankee owners Dan Topping and Del Webb decided it was time to leave baseball. They sold their Yankee ownership to the Columbia Broadcasting System. CBS installed a former World War II OSS agent and successful network executive, dapper Michael Burke, as president of the club.

Burke could see the Yankees needed changes. Mantle, Ford, Berra, and Maris were on the down sides of their careers. He began by retiring Yogi as a player and naming him as manager of the club. Ralph Houk was moved up to general manager.

Berra had been a comical character around the Yankees since 1947 when he first joined the team. His legendary remarks, popularized in many cases by St. Louis neighborhood pal and big-league catcher Joe Garagiola, were repeated often—as they are to this day.

"Thank you for making this day necessary," Yogi told the crowd at Yankee Stadium when he was honored.

"Nobody goes there any more. It's too crowded," he told friends when asked about a popular restaurant.

"It ain't over till it's over," he said when asked about a tight pennant race in his later career as a Mets manager when he led that team to a National League championship in 1973.

He was liked by everybody. Nobody doubted his baseball knowledge. What many doubted at the beginning of his managerial career in 1964 was his ability to handle the Yankees, especially the other veteran players he had been so close to for so many years.

The Yankees bounced in and out of first place most of the 1964 season. In August Mantle suffered another foot injury. Maris moved to center field. He played brilliantly. The fans hardly cared. They missed the Mick.

In late August the Yankees were five games out of first place. They lost a doubleheader in Chicago. Even the usually cheerful younger players—Bouton, Tresh, Pepitone, and Linz—were in a silent, sullen mood.

It was a steamy hot day. The Yankee players walked slowly to the team bus for the ride to the airport and a flight to Boston for the next night's game.

The bus was an overused school bus with narrow seats and no air conditioning. The players, anxious for a cold beer and an air-conditioned plane ride to Boston, grew edgy.

The bus pulled out of Comiskey Park. Chicago fans hooted at the Yankee players as they opened the windows. Nothing was more popular to rowdy fans in every city in the league than screaming at the Yankees when they were down. They had won too often to suit diehard fans in other towns.

All conditions were ripe for an explosion.

As the bus moved lazily down Outer Drive in Chicago toward O'Hare Airport, backup shortstop Phil Linz, who had been playing regularly since shortstop Tony Kubek was injured, pulled a harmonica from his pocket. He had purchased the harmonica early that day to play in his room.

"There was a lot of tension on that bus. I thought I could relieve some of it by playing a little tune. The only one I knew was 'Mary Had a Little Lamb,'" said Linz.

Linz played the tune slowly on his harmonica. Since it was the only tune he knew, he played it over and over.

Yogi Berra was in the front seat of the bus. Coach Frank Crosetti, who had started as a Yankee shortstop in 1932 and had been with the team as a player and coach ever since, was next to Yogi.

Linz was in a seat near the back of the steamy bus. Joe Pepitone was sitting next to him. Mickey Mantle and Whitey Ford were in the last two seats of the bus.

As Linz played "Mary Had a Little Lamb" for perhaps the fifteenth time, Crosetti turned in his seat and told Linz to stop playing. Linz ignored him.

"You're a disgrace to the Yankees," Crosetti shouted.

Linz answered by playing some more.

Now Berra, fed up with the playing and the hollering, got up from his seat. He said something which Linz was not quite able to hear.

Linz turned to Mantle. "What did he say?" he asked Mickey.

"Play louder," said Mantle.

Linz did as he was told.

Now Berra, totally outraged at what he saw as insubordination, told Linz to quit playing.

Linz, for no explainable reason, flipped the harmonica to Berra. Yogi grabbed it, catching it as he caught everything thrown at him. He fired it back toward Linz.

The harmonica hit Pepitone on the knee. He immediately began screaming in mock pain.

"*My knee, my knee,*" he yelled. "*Get the doc...my knee!*"

There was no way the lightweight harmonica could have damaged him.

"To this day, I don't know why I threw the harmonica at Yogi," said Linz recently.

"I liked Yogi. He was good to me. I guess it was a hot day and we were all fed up with losing."

Berra and Crosetti screamed at Linz and Pepitone. Mantle and Ford covered their faces. There was a general release of tension.

At the airport, I called my office and dictated a story about the incident. It made the front page of the *Post*.

In Boston the next evening, dozens of reporters filled the clubhouse. Berra said he would fine Linz $200 for the incident after Linz apologized. Everyone relaxed. The next day Linz negotiated a $10,000 endorsement contract with a harmonica company.

With Maris playing a wonderful center field in place of the injured Mantle and Linz playing brilliantly in place of Kubek, the Yankees went on to win the pennant again.

For the fifth straight year, they would be in the World Series. No one could have guessed that their next attempt would not come until twelve years later, in 1976.

Mantle was feeling strong again by the time the World Series against the St. Louis Cardinals opened in St. Louis on October 7, 1964. His old pal, Yogi Berra, that lovable elf, had led the Yankees back from a midsummer slump to a close pennant victory over the Chicago White Sox.

The Cardinals had been involved in one of the strangest pennant races in baseball history. Many sportswriters look back on that National League pennant race and call it "the Year of the Great Choke."

Philadelphia, under tyrannical skipper Gene Mauch, led by six and a half games, with ten games to go. They had two of the finest pitchers on their staff—left-hander Chris Short and Jim Bunning, later to become a Kentucky congressman and a perfect game pitcher against the Mets that year.

Bunning won 19 games that year. Short won 17. Because Bunning couldn't get to 20 wins and Short couldn't get to 18, the Phillies couldn't hang on to first place.

Each of them pitched twice with only two days of rest in the last week of the season as Mauch tried to lock up the pennant. Each lost.

The Phillies blew the pennant, and the Cardinals snuck in after losing the first two games of a weekend series to the lowly New York Mets.

Bob Gibson started the Friday night game and relieved in the Sunday game as the Cardinals wrapped it up. He would later emerge as the star of the Series, and though tired, manager Johnny Keane allowed him to lock up the last game. When asked by reporters why he stayed with Gibson when he had fresh relief arms in the bullpen, he replied, "I have a commitment to his heart."

The Cards won the first game of the Series behind left-hander Ray Sadecki and relief pitcher Barney Schultz, a thirty-eight-year-old knuckleball expert from Beverly, New Jersey. The Yankees came back behind rookie Mel Stottlemyre to win the second game 8-3.

The third game, before a tense Yankee Stadium crowd of 67,101, proved to be one of the best Series games in a long time—one of the most dramatic of Mickey's career and one of his favorite memories.

Left-hander Curt Simmons started for St. Louis, and right-hander Jim Bouton, an overachieving smallish right-hander, started for New York.

Bouton was one of the brightest, wittiest, liveliest baseball players of his time. He won 21 games in 1963 and 18 in 1964. He was more friendly with sportswriters, who he felt challenged him intellectually, than with most of his teammates.

He later wrote an iconoclastic baseball book entitled *Ball Four*, with *New York Post* curmudgeon sportswriter Leonard Shecter. The book was a best-seller, a smash, because it revealed baseball intimacies about life on the road.

One line in the book cost Bouton dearly. He suggested Mantle might even have achieved more in his career if he didn't bend his elbow so much.

Mantle was stung by the public pronouncement of his until then private drinking habits. The Yankees reacted by banning Bouton for life from the Stadium Old Timer events.

In 1993 when Mickey's son Billy died of a heart attack at the age of thirty-six, Bouton sent a condolence note. It was only then that the tension between the two men eased.

"Mickey called and left a message on my answering machine thanking me for the note. 'Jim, this is Mick.' He went on to say he appreciated my note and never really held it against me for writing what I did," Bouton said in 1995.

On this 1964 afternoon, before this huge crowd, Bouton was marvelous. Pitching with intense concentration so hard that his hat kept falling off on almost every pitch, his less than heavyweight body hurtling forward to the plate, he kept the Cardinals to one run through nine innings.

Simmons, who had actually knocked in the St. Louis run with a single off Bouton, was just as good through eight innings.

Keane decided to pinch-hit for Simmons in the ninth. The Cardinals failed to break the tie.

Barney Schultz became the St. Louis pitcher in the bottom of the ninth. Mantle was the first hitter.

"I hated batting against knuckleball pitchers," said Mantle year later. "They could tie you up and make you look terrible."

The crowd never could have imagined that Mantle, their great hero, was actually insecure about facing Schultz as the leadoff hitter in the ninth inning.

He moved slowly to the plate, carrying three bats. He dropped one as he left the dugout and dropped the second as he neared the plate.

He pumped his 38-inch, 36-ounce bat as he faced Schultz. He stood deep in the batter's box, his eyes fixed on the mound, his spikes dug into the dirt, his shoulders slightly hunched, his elbows held tightly.

There was a strange mixture of anticipation and silence from the huge crowd at the Stadium. This was a common occurrence whenever Mantle came to the plate. First there was the air of approval from the crowd as the broad-backed man with the large number seven on his uniform shirt walked in. Then there was silence.

It was a bit eerie. Thousands waited breathlessly as Mantle took aim. It was their hope to once again see a lifelong cherished event, the historic swing, the one blow that would link them forever with their handsome blonde hero.

Mantle always held the bat relatively still at the plate when he was set. There were no awkward motions, no theatrics, no attempts to intimidate the pitcher with a pointed charge at him.

Schultz threw eight warm-up pitches to catcher Tim McCarver. Each one danced and dipped and delayed its arrival at the plate.

Mantle bit down on his lower lip, as he often did, and studied his man.

Schultz looked in at McCarver. The young catcher put down three fingers—no surprise, the signal for a knuckleball. McCarver also thought about not being intimidated by Schultz's knuckler, a pitch that would often make a catcher look as bad as a defeated hitter.

Schultz brought his hands over his head and threw the first pitch to home plate. It was a knuckleball that seemed to take forever to get there.

Mantle waited, waited, waited. Then he swung left-handed and connected as the ball finally reached the plate. It was driven on a high arch to the deepest part of the right-field stands, some 450 feet from home plate, arriving there at the instant Mantle began his jog toward first base.

The Yankee bench leaped from the dugout. Mantle, his head down, his eyes focused on the Stadium dirt, his legs moving with that slight limp he always exhibited now, ran his home run home.

Elston Howard, the next Yankee batter, shook Mantle's hand warmly at home plate, patted him on the back, and squeezed his neck.

By now, all of the Yankees were around the home plate area as Mantle moved through a crowd of his teammates. He wore a huge grin.

The World Series home run, which won the game 2-1 for the Yankees, was Mantle's 16th Series homer. He had passed Ruth in that regard. He hit another homer in the sixth game and a final Series home run, his 18th, in the seventh game.

Ted Williams had left the game after hitting his last home run in 1960 off young Baltimore pitcher Jack Fisher. Mantle always wanted it to end that way for him. It didn't. It would have been so mystical, so marvelous, so dramatic if Mickey had quit after that homer.

Years later he would talk of that home run off Schultz in the third game of the World Series as one of the most emotional events of his career. For those fans in attendance, there would never be a baseball thrill to rival it.

Mantle got his last Series home run off Bob Gibson in the seventh game. The Yankees trailed 7-3 in the final game when Clete Boyer, the third baseman, and Phil Linz, the harmonica-playing shortstop, homered off Gibson.

Keane, an emotional man, stayed with his game pitcher instead of going to Schultz again for the final out. He, too, may have been moved by Mantle's superb home run.

Bobby Richardson was the next batter after Linz. Then Roger Maris and Mickey Mantle waited to steal the game and the Series.

Gibson ran the count to 2-2 on Richardson as the St. Louis crowd held its breath. Then he threw a fastball down the middle of the plate. Richardson, who had 13 hits that Series and batted .406, popped up to shortstop Dal Maxvill.

It was the end of the Series, and although Mantle could not know it then, it was the end of his World Series experiences.

The sadness in that Yankee clubhouse was much less intense than it had been in previous losing clubhouses in 1963 and 1960. The Yankees understood that the Cardinals were simply a better team.

Mantle, Ford, Maris, and Elston Howard were on their way out. It was an aging Yankee team now with aging stars. Rookie manager Yogi Berra was also on the way out as skipper, though he was unaware of it at that time.

The next afternoon Johnny Keane quit as St. Louis manager, and Yogi Berra was fired as the Yankee manager.

Keane left because his pal, Bing Devine, had been fired as Cardinals general manager. Keane also knew that the owner, Gussie Busch, had offered Keane's managerial job to Leo Durocher.

Yankee general manager Ralph Houk, an old minor-league pal, had quietly contacted Keane late during the previous August. Keane's daughter revealed this information to Yankees first baseman Joe Pepitone while they frolicked on a Florida beach together the following spring.

Pepitone passed this information on to sports columnist Milton Gross, and it was splashed on the front pages of the *Post* shortly after Keane was hired by the Yankees to succeed Berra.

The Yankees had flown home after the losing seventh game of the Series. Berra had been summoned to the offices of Dan Topping—still the nominal owner until CBS officially took over—for an afternoon meeting.

Berra was certain a new long-term contract was in the offing. After all, he had rallied the club from its midsummer slump to a pennant and a seven-game World Series, even though it had ended in defeat.

Instead, Topping and Houk told Yogi he was not being rehired. They offered him a job as a Yankee scout. He told them he'd think it over. Two weeks later he left the Yankees to take a job as a Mets coach under Casey Stengel.

The end of the 1964 season was a sad time for Mickey Mantle. He was well aware that his talents were eroding. He could see fastballs he used to cream getting past him. With the exception of Whitey Ford, who was having his own difficulties with his pitching arm, he was alone most of the time on the team. He was surrounded by younger team members, with whom he had less in common. Their stars were on the rise, his was waning.

The 1965 spring training was an anxious time for Mantle.

Johnny Keane, the new manager, was a small man with deep-set eyes in a narrow face and closely cropped hair . The first manager since Casey Stengel, in 1949, who had not been a part of the Yankees in some capacity, he seemed out of his element as he surveyed the team.

True superstars of the game, Mantle and Ford, were losing their skills, but still remained the most significant presences on the team.

Few chores are as difficult for a baseball manager as the easing out of a star when he is no longer able to offer peak performance.

It happened with Babe Ruth and Miller Huggins, with Joe DiMaggio and Casey Stengel, with Bob Feller and Al Lopez, with Warren Spahn and Casey Stengel, and to Casey Stengel as a manager.

Spahn, the winningest left-hander in baseball history, had broken in with the Boston Braves in 1942 and ended his career with the Mets and San Francisco Giants in 1965. Stengel had been the Braves manager in 1942, and in Spahn's final days in 1965, he was managing with the Mets.

"I played for Casey before and after he was a genius," Spahn liked to remark.

In 1942 the Braves were a horrible team. The Mets in 1965 were equally bad. Spahn didn't pitch much in 1942 because he was inexperienced. He missed pitching much in 1965 because he was finished.

Keane quickly saw that he would have the same kind of problem with Mantle and Ford. They were definitely headed for the Hall of Fame in the future, but for the present they were two aging, injured, tired baseball players.

Keane was also rather laconic—an introverted man who seemed clinically depressed most of the time. He took poorly to the shenanigans of Mantle and Ford during spring training.

Mantle and Ford may have been losing their baseball skills, but they still enjoyed a laugh, a practical joke, a rousing night out on the town. Neither believed there was any connection between what they did after midnight with what they did during daylight hours.

It wasn't Keane's way. He expected undivided attention and unsurpassed dedication from all his players—and that meant Mantle and Ford as well as all the rest.

What seemed to be more significant, and probably always is in baseball, was that Keane was truly jealous of Mantle and Ford. He had no playing career to speak of. He had never made it to the big leagues and was always interested in imposing his will on those who had.

He saw himself as an incredibly moral man in a world of louts.

When the New York press refused to believe that he had had no contact with the Yankees before he quit in St. Louis, Keane was damaged emotionally. When his own daughter confirmed that he had indeed spoken to the Yankees and when it became known that he was aware that he would have a job waiting if he quit St. Louis, the serious face of his morality play on his resignation became a comical farce.

"He just never communicated with Whitey and me," said Mantle. "He just stared at us. I knew that I would never get along with this guy."

If Keane was to win over the Yankees to his way of doing things, he would have to win over Mantle.

It would never happen.

Pitcher Steve Hamilton presents Mickey with a plaque that commemorates his 500th home run. The plaque hangs at the spot in Yankee Stadium where Mantle hit the homer.

MICKEY MANTLE

ON MAY 14, 1967 MICKEY MANTLE'S 500TH LIFETIME HOME RUN LANDED HERE. MICKEY BECAME THE SIXTH PLAYER IN BASEBALL HISTORY TO HIT 500 HOMERS. HIT OFF STU MILLER AS YANKEES BEAT BALTIMORE, 6-5

The End

I*f Hollywood had created the Mickey Mantle story, they would have had the legendary Mickey quit baseball after his 1964 World Series home run off St. Louis knuckleballer Barney Schultz. That would have been the ultimate in drama and excitement.*

Instead, he labored through four more years.

Mickey never really had a good season after 1964. His average dropped to an embarrassing .255 in 1965, crept up to .288 in 1966, then dropped to .245, and finally to .237.

The last two seasons of his career cost him dearly. Because of them, his lifetime .300 mark dropped to a career average of .298. He often told me that his lifetime batting average was the biggest disappointment of his career.

"That really hurts," he said of the .298 figure. "I belonged up there with the lifetime .300 hitters. I know now I should have quit earlier."

The 1965 season got off on the wrong foot for Mantle and Whitey Ford. It went bad even faster as the two aging stars chafed under the uptight managerial style of Johnny Keane.

In the spring of 1965, Mantle kidded with a sportswriter about playing center field, and having to chase down all of Whitey's pitching mistakes. The sportswriter, an aging relic himself, and almost always under the influence of alcohol, wrote the joking remarks as a serious story.

He suggested that Whitey and Mickey were feuding, that Johnny Keane was feuding with both of them, and that all the players were rebeling against Keane. There was a little bit of truth to what he said.

The story made big headlines back in New York. It soured Keane on the press covering the Yankees for the rest of his time with the team.

The Yankees had lost their desire to win. Mantle and Ford were at the end of their careers. Maris was hurting. The new youngsters were inadequate for the job, and the pressures on Keane were terrible.

At the same time, the New York Mets were becoming the darlings of the town.

In July of that year, Casey Stengel was injured in a fall on Old Timer's Day during a party at Toots Shor's restaurant. He had to retire.

His faithful coach, Wes Westrum, became the new manager. Westrum got nothing but sympathy from the fans—especially when he botched the English language, as he frequently did.

Westrum continually called a close game a cliff dweller instead of a cliff-hanger. He mispronounced the names of most of the players and moaned after losses, "Wasn't that awful?"

Sportswriters who had enjoyed their years with Casey now shifted their affections to Westrum and his management of the Mets.

New York fans turned away from the Yankees as the Bronx Bombers slipped from the heights and turned in increasing numbers to the four-year-old legend in the making, the Mets.

Mantle and Keane hardly spoke to each other. Mickey hit an occasional homer, but also took an occasional day off when his legs were bothering him badly.

After five straight pennants, the 1965 season ended with the Yankees in sixth place, with a 77-85 record.

Again in 1966 the team got off to a poor start. Keane was befuddled. Joe Pepitone, the rowdy first baseman, actually had the audacity to date Keane's daughter during spring training. This put the manager in an even more delicate position when he tried to discipline the immature and unreliable Pepitone.

Rumors quickly began to circulate that Keane was about to be fired.

One Friday night while the team was in Anaheim, California, for a game against the Los Angeles Angels, Keane sat in the hotel lobby. As I walked over to speak with him, I saw a man whose eyes looked sunken deep in their sockets. He was unshaven. He looked wrinkled and haggard.

In a voice that was barely above a whisper, he asked me, "What do you hear?"

The next morning he heard for himself, firsthand. He had been fired. Ralph Houk was coming back on the field as manager. Lee MacPhail would run the club from upstairs.

"He just wasn't the man for the job," Mantle later said.

Even under Houk, it quickly became evident that the Yankees were going downhill rapidly. It wasn't the manager's fault. It was lack of talent. The team quickly sank to tenth place in the new expanded ten-team setup, and stayed there.

Part of the problem this time around was that Houk was managing differently. Older now, he had lost much of his fire. He felt he had already proved his worth. Now he began to run a more relaxed team and let many players get away with too much.

When I suggested in a *New York Post* column that the skipper was softer now than in his previous time at the helm, and that even he could not squash the frivolity of Pepitone and other rowdy young players, he confronted me in the clubhouse. He saw the article as an attack on his manliness. I knew then Houk would never invite me to his retirement party.

Mantle revived a bit under Houk, managed 23 homers, and got his average back up to a respectable .288.

In 1967 Houk decided he could save some of the wear and tear on Mickey and possibly lengthen his career by playing him at first base. Pepitone was moved to center field, and Mantle went to first base.

Pepitone was very fast and graceful in the outfield—when he wanted to be. He didn't want to be very often.

Mantle was good enough at first base if he was hitting well, but he wasn't hitting well. Now he was hurting the team at bat and not helping them in the field.

Still, there were some glorious moments along the way. On May 14, 1967, he hit his 500th home run off Stu Miller of Baltimore. Babe Ruth finished with 714. It was unlikely Mickey would challenge that record, but a fellow named Hank Aaron might. He was still at the top of his game.

On July 4, 1967, Mickey hit two homers off Jim "Mudcat" Grant in Minnesota. He hit six home runs in the last eleven weeks of the season.

At home over that winter he considered quitting. He was in a lot of pain. He was dealing with new problems in his shoulders and legs. He had lost his enthusiasm for the game, and he was lonely now during the season. Whitey Ford had quit in May with a circulatory problem in his shoulder.

With nobody to hang out with after games, he decided that 1968 would be his final season. He was undecided about his future after baseball.

Mantle seemed more relaxed in spring training in 1968. He told no one of his decision to retire, but all the evidence was there. He was more sociable around the batting cage, easier for the press to talk to, easier to approach after losses. He hardly ever hid in the trainer's room now. He actually enjoyed kidding with sportswriters like myself, who had covered him a decade earlier when he was at his peak.

Occasionally, he hit a huge batting-practice home run. I would joke with him that Bill Fischer must have thrown that one. He had hit the huge blast against the facade off of Fischer in 1963. He would chuckle as he heard me tell other younger sportswriters about that blast five years earlier.

"I hit the fuh-card," he would say in a loud voice. The two of us would laugh together over the memory.

On May 6, 1968, he homered off left-hander Sam McDowell, the strikeout star of the Cleveland Indians. It was another in a long line of meaningless Yankee games in the late 1960s, but for Mantle the hit had great meaning. This was career home run number 522.

The Stadium crowd went wild as Yankee public relations director Bob Fishel posted the number on the electronic scoreboard: 522. Those numbers sat out there several feet high.

"It just gave me chills," Mantle said after the game. "To think that I had passed my hero, Ted Williams, in home runs was really thrilling. I couldn't get over it."

Mantle confessed that many warm memories had whirled through his head that day—World Series home runs, big hits, All-Star games, exciting pennant races. One thought dominated all others.

"I just kept thinking how proud my dad would have been of me," he said quietly.

The Yankees asked Mantle not to make a final decision about quitting and certainly not to tell the press anything.

Once the regular season started, it was a different story. Mantle now began spending more and more time in the clubhouse before games and less time on the field.

Marty Appel, currently the publicity director for Topps, was then the assistant public relations director with the Yankees in 1968. He worked under Bob Fishel, who had started in baseball with Bill Veeck in Cleveland twenty years earlier.

"Hundreds of handwritten letters and drawings arrived at the Stadium each day, addressed to Mickey," Appel recalled. "Most said

In the twilight of his career Mantle traded in his out-fielder's glove for a first baseman's mitt.

'You're my favorite player. May I have your autograph?' There was a quality of politeness and a respect in their request. I would save up my little folder of important mail and wait for a good time to meet with him. Often that was during batting practice, which, I was shocked to note, Mickey often skipped.

"I never asked him why, but clearly the wear and tear on his legs required a rationing of his time. I hoped it wasn't because he didn't feel like part of the team, but in fact, he was the last of the great ones left," said Appel.

"I came to realize that his own teammates were as in awe of him as I was. Many times the players would come to me—not him—and ask if a photo could be arranged with him. We always got the job done," Appel said.

Bobby Cox, manager of the 1995 World Champion Altanta Braves , was a utility infielder with the Yankees in 1968. He was one of the players who asked Appel to arrange a photo with Mantle. That picture could be seen on his wall at Atlanta's Fulton County Stadium when Cox was being doused with champagne after his team's Series victory.

The affection and reverence that teammates had for Mantle was so deep, so strong, so honest, that it could not be measured. Many had autographed photos of him on the walls of their dens at home. Most of them—especially those that played with him in his later years—had collected bats, balls, hats, gloves, uniforms, and jackets with his autograph on them.

More than twenty of his teammates from the late 1950s through his last year in 1968 named their own children after him. Family days at Yankee Stadium were filled with wide-eyed youngsters—Mickey Gibbs, Mickey Tresh, Mickey Closter, Mickey Bahnsen, Mickey Cumberland to name just a few.

Most ballplayers put on a show of being tough guys with a professional air. They keep a wall of silence around their emotions, but even they will become emotional in the face of heroism by legendary baseball figures they have come to revere.

For all his accomplishments, for all his ease and openness with them, Mickey Mantle was one of the most beloved players among his colleagues.

"There was never any air of being a big shot," said old pal Whitey Ford. "Mickey just liked being part of the club. The guys were quick to see that about him."

As the Yankees visited each city that year, local sportswriters suggested that this might be the last time the fans would see Mantle.

Crowds came out and cheered his every at-bat. Sportswriters filled the pages of their newspapers with reminiscences about him. Often players from opposing teams gathered around him as he took the field. They shook his hand, wished him well, and told him how much they would miss seeing him.

Many players said to him, "You were my childhood hero." He found it embarrassing.

He had been around the American League 18 seasons by then. Many of the players he was now facing were five or six years old when he started to play. The passage of time has a humbling effect on a baseball player.

The most celebrated player of 1968 was a right-handed pitcher on the Detroit Tigers by the name of Denny McLain.

McLain was a free spirit, a guy who played by his own rules, an amusing character in a world of straight shooters, and he was having an historic season.

No pitcher had won 30 games in big-league baseball since Dizzy Dean in 1934. It was a mark of such excellence that many observers thought it might never happen again.

On September 19, McLain was winning his 29th game of the year. He had the Yankees beaten 6-0. He had two more starts and would win both of them to finish with 31 victories. Nobody has won 30 games since.

On that evening, Mantle walked to the plate in the ninth inning. The Detroit crowd, realizing that this could be Mickey's final at-bat in one of the best baseball cities in the league, gave him a huge ovation.

As he strolled to the plate, McLain walked in off the mound to talk to his catcher, Bill Freehan. Freehan was a former college star at the University of Michigan who had become a big Tiger hero.

On this occasion McLain, the son-in-law of former Cleveland Indians shortstop and manager Lou Boudreau, wanted to give one of his heroes a gift.

In a stage whisper loud enough for Mickey to hear, McLain said to Freehan, "I'm gonna let Mickey hit one."

He had the game won. He was having a great career year. He could do no wrong. The event would not impact on the game except for a single score.

It is one of baseball's little secrets that ballplayers often help their pals on opposing teams. There are many occasions, in games already lost, when a pitcher will deliver an easy pitch for a pal. An infielder may move slowly for a ground ball hit by a buddy, or an outfielder will move away from the wall when a former teammate hits a questionable long fly ball.

It is only human. And it has been going on since the game was invented.

Mantle asked Freehan if what he had heard McLain say about giving him an easy pitch to hit was accurate. He wanted to be certain he wasn't being set up to crowd the plate, only to have a fastball buzz his ears. Freehan assured him it was legitimate.

Mantle stood at the plate as the first pitch came in at batting-practice speed. Nothing on it, right down the center of the plate.

McLain, a right-hander, was throwing Mantle a pitch out over the plate. Pitchers had avoided throwing Mantle a pitch in that area when he batted left-handed for the past eighteen years.

The next pitch was in the same area, maybe a little higher, and Mantle swung viciously. He was under the pitch a bit, and it curled back foul against the screen behind home plate.

Even in the big leagues, even with hitters as skilled as Mickey Mantle, hitting a pitched ball over a distant fence is not that easy. If it were, there would be nothing but home runs hit in batting practice.

Players collect at batting cages all over big-league ballparks and compete for home runs. They might bet a drink, a dinner, a date with the other guy's girl friend—on long home run hits. If they get eight or ten batting-practice pitches, they might hit one or two out of the park—if they are lucky. The other pitched balls will be dribblers, fouls, soft line drives, a long ball that falls short of the fence, or a huge pop-up.

It just isn't that easy.

Now the pitcher was ready for his next throw.

In a normal game, with the pitcher working the hitter, the next thrown ball would be high and inside, low and outside, or fired across the plate as a surprise.

Few hitters actually swing at the 0-2 pitch because most pitchers tend to throw balls that can not even be reached. One of the cardinal sins of baseball is for a pitcher to give up a big hit, especially a long-ball home run, on a 0-2 pitch.

Mantle stood at home plate and dug in. He motioned with his hand that he would like the pitch a bit higher than the one he had just fouled off. McLain smiled. Then he nodded from the mound.

This was a different situation. This was Denny McLain having a magnificent year, facing Mickey Mantle, finishing up a magnificent career.

The ball came in letter high, about 85 miles an hour, right in the area of the plate that Mantle had always concentrated on.

He swung viciously, as he almost always did, and the crack of the bat against the ball resonated throughout the ballpark.

I stood up from my seat in the press box and watched the ball go out. We all knew that it was a prearranged pitch. There was no doubt about that among any of the sportswriters, the fans who were there, or the players who watched the event from the dugout.

Mantle's 535th career home run crashed against the seats in the upper stands at Tiger Stadium.

Mantle had a huge smile on his face as he ran around the bases. He never looked at McLain as he came around until he passed third base. The noise of the cheering fans, many of whom noticed the byplay, was deafening.

Mantle tipped his cap as he neared home plate and subtly glanced over at McLain on the mound. McLain saw Mantle's gesture to the fans as a greeting to him as well. McLain pulled the cap off his head, held it over his head for a moment, and in a sweeping motion, put it back on.

If I were measuring historic Mantle home runs, the one off McLain sits up there with the Stobbs tape measure job, the World Series homer off Barney Schultz, the Bill Fischer "fah-card" job, and the comeback 1963 homer off George Brunet. (Mantle always voted for the Schultz homer as his favorite because it won a World Series game on one swing.)

The next night the Yankees played the Boston Red Sox at the Stadium. Jim Lonborg was the pitcher. He became a Boston World Series hero in 1967 when they came so close against the Cardinals. After his baseball career was over, he would go on to a successful career in dentistry. During 1967 he was busy winning 22 games. In 1968 he pitched with a bad arm and was having trouble. He couldn't throw very hard.

The day after the McLain home run, Mantle was facing Lonborg, another right-hander, at Yankee Stadium.

The crowd had read the stories in the New York newspapers that day about the Detroit home run. They practically begged Lonborg to do the same thing as they screamed, "Lay it in, lay it in!"

Lonborg would hear of no such thing. He retired Mickey on a pop-up in the first inning.

In the fourth inning, Mantle caught one of Lonborg's not-so-fast fastballs and drove it into the right-field stands.

It wasn't one of Mickey's hardest hit home runs, not one of his highest, certainly not one of his more dramatic, and not one of winning significance.

It was historic all the same.

That was the final home run of Mickey's career—number 536—and it only became significant because he hit no other home runs in the remaining eight games of the season.

History is often hard to recognize when it is happening. I sat in the

Mantle called it quits in 1968,
almost as boyish-looking as
when he started in 1951.

Yankees press box that day, recorded the home run in my score book, and made no special mention of it in my game story.

Although there were indications that Mantle might retire after that season, nothing was definite. There was always a possibility that Mickey would hit another homer—maybe two or three more—before the season ended with McLain and the Tigers going on to a World Series triumph.

Little fuss was made in the clubhouse after that homer because the Yankees lost the game 4-3. Lonborg beat a young Yankee left-hander named Fritz Peterson.

There were eight games to go. Mantle played in six of them. His average continued to sink. On the final Friday night of the season, in Boston, Mantle faced Lonborg again. He hit a pop fly to shortstop Rico Petrocelli, limped toward first, and returned to the dugout.

Manager Ralph Houk sensed that the burden of being Mickey Mantle in this abysmal season was too much for him. Without asking Mickey, Houk sent Andy Kosco out to play first base.

It was over.

Mantle's career ended with a whimper, not a bang.

Nothing much was made of this because the actual retirement event would not be held until March of 1969 at the Yankees training camp in Fort Lauderdale, Florida.

Mickey knew he could no longer fool anyone, especially himself. He hated to walk away from the money. He did not have the flair for making money or, perhaps, choosing a good manager to handle his salary for him. He had not accumulated enough cash through the years to retire with ease. Unfortunately, he had no choice.

The baseball community was involved in serious labor negotiations in the spring of 1969. There was talk of a strike.

Steve Hamilton, the player representative of the Yankees, called Mantle that winter at home in Dallas. Hamilton, a lanky pitcher, was known as "the Bone."

"Mick, the Bone calling," he said.

"How you doing?"

"We have a favor to ask, Mickey. If you are retiring, could you hold off on the announcement until the spring? It would help our negotiations to know you are with us."

"I wasn't planning anything until I get down there," he said.

Mantle had actually made up his mind to come to spring training for a while, work out a bit, and then decide about his future.

As the snow fell in New York and Mantle played with his kids in Texas, he was close to making the decision.

He put on the Yankee uniform in spring training next February. He knew that he would not play another game wearing it. After a few days of hitting lightly, running easily, and throwing with pain, he told Ralph Houk that he was going home for good.

The Yankees called a press conference at the ballpark for March 1, 1969. It was for the New York sportswriters on the beat, a few Florida writers, and a couple of television cameras. It was just about the smallest turnout for a Mickey Mantle press conference I could ever remember.

That was just the way Mickey wanted it.

The next time I saw him was June 8, 1969. That was the year the Mets won the World Series, men walked on the moon, and Mickey Mantle's uniform number seven was retired.

It was a glorious Saturday afternoon in late spring. Michael Burke, who ran the Yankees, arranged for Mantle, DiMaggio, scout Tom Greenwade, Mantle's first manager Harry Craft, George Selkirk, several dozen teammates, and the Mantle family to be on hand for the ceremony.

Mantle had always been a bit standoffish with fans. He acknowledged their cheers as a player on occasion, tipped his hat, waved after a big home run. He was not a guy who hung around the fences signing autographs and exchanging funny stories with strangers.

On this afternoon broadcaster Mel Allen, who had been fired by the Yankees after the 1964 season, came back to the Stadium for the first time. The man who had been on the field for the retirement of uniforms for Lou Gehrig, Babe Ruth, and Joe DiMaggio was now presiding over the retirement of Mantle's number seven. Mel Allen had always been a fan favorite, and Burke understood his historic link to the Yankees past.

"That magnificent Yankee, number seven, Mickey Mantle," Allen intoned in his Alabama drawl.

Mantle walked to microphones that had been placed near home plate. The noise was deafening. On and on it went—cheers, whistles, screams, endless applause. Mantle seemed overwhelmed as he stood alone before sixty thousand people. He stared straight ahead and tears welled up in his eyes. The outpourings of love and devotion continued. Ten minutes passed.

Each time Mantle waved to the crowd and moved closer to the microphones to start talking, the crowd increased the volume of their cheers. It was as though the fans had decided they would thank him in this most public of ways for the joy his career had given them, and no one, not even Mantle himself, could take that pleasure from them.

As Yankee executives and Mantle family members moved restlessly about on the field behind Mickey, Michael Burke finally got the crowd to quiet down when he suggested they would never hear Mickey speak if they continued with their applause.

Mantle began by suggesting that on his retirement day another plaque should be given to DiMaggio, because he had admired him and learned so much from him. It was a wonderful gesture to make, but there was not one bit of truth in it. Then he thanked the Yankees, Casey Stengel, and all his teammates. He said now he understood Lou Gehrig's phrase about being the "luckiest man on the face of the earth."

For the first time in his life, Mantle seemed to recognize his impact on perfect strangers. He knew his teammates loved, admired, and even worshipped him. He knew fans always cheered his homers. On this day, after eighteen Yankee seasons, he finally accepted and came to understand his stature in their eyes. They saw him as a sort of god among men.

He was thirty seven years old that afternoon. He was in good health, still wickedly handsome with that short blonde hair and those piercing blue eyes and the beautifully muscled body of the well-conditioned athlete. He was also emotionally spent.

When he began talking about how different the Stadium felt and looked, it must have seemed very strange to him. He stood there, not in his Yankee uniform but dressed in his dark blue suit and highly polished dress shoes.

"That had to be one of the highlights of my life," he told me years later. "I never stopped crying. It was as if I was a stranger out there, as if the years I played were part of somebody else's career."

He also talked about a recurring dream he had that first spring of his retirement. It was one he would have for many years afterwards.

"In my dream I would be in a cab, arriving at the Stadium as the game was starting. I would hear my name being announced and the crowds roaring. All the gates were locked. I couldn't get in. I would start running all around the entrances. No one was there. No one could let me in. I bent down low and tried to crawl under a gate like a child. Still I couldn't get in. Finally I would wake up in a terrible sweat," he said.

No one can separate himself from his life's work of eighteen years, as Mantle had to do that afternoon, without great difficulty. "That's really the moment when I realized it was over," he said years later. "I would never play again. I would never be part of the Yankees. I would never hang around the clubhouse, kidding with the other guys. I had to move on. It wasn't easy."

When he returned home after the ceremonies, he wandered around his home in Dallas. He played golf, watched television, read the sports pages. He spent time with his kids and attended an occasional banquet. He made a few commercials.

He soon became involved in a restaurant deal—Mickey Mantle's Country Cookin'—with franchises throughout Oklahoma and Texas.

It looked good on paper, but the business went bust in a hurry.

He tried opening a bowling alley. Yogi had done the same, and it had been a great success. He got involved in a chain of motels. He tried a little television broadcasting for NBC. He was only mildly successful.

In 1970 Ralph Houk asked him to come to spring training and work with some of the kids. If he liked the job, he could stay on as a Yankee coach.

He didn't like it very much.

"Most of the time nobody took me very seriously as a coach," he said. "They only wanted to talk about some home run I hit, or pose for a picture for their collection. I felt uncomfortable."

He became involved in an insurance company, playing golf with clients and meeting with agents. He talked about his home runs and tried to inspire them to do their best for the company. Everyone wanted a picture taken with Mantle, and none of them could remember a word he said after he autographed their photos.

Through the early 1970s, we would run into each other at sports banquets, New York City charity events, Yankee promotions, or at the New York Baseball Writers Dinner.

We reminisced about some of his favorite home runs or spoke about some of his teammates. His laugh was always hearty and his manner always upbeat.

Once in a while he would talk about his standing in the game and actually asked me if I thought the lifetime average under .300 would hurt his chances in the Hall of Fame voting. I told him not to worry about that. He would be a lock for election.

Mantle was inducted into the Hall of Fame on August 12, 1974. He made it along with pal Whitey Ford, a Negro League star named James "Cool Papa" Bell, and umpire Jocko Conlan.

He stood before a crowd of 10,000 people on the steps of the Hall of Fame library in Cooperstown, New York, and acknowledged his acceptance.

Commissioner Bowie Kuhn read from his plaque:

MICKEY CHARLES MANTLE
NEW YORK AL 1951–1968
HIT 536 HOME RUNS. WON LEAGUE HOME RUN TITLE AND SLUGGING CROWN FOUR TIMES. MADE 2415 HITS. BATTED .300 OR OVER IN EACH OF TEN YEARS WITH TOP OF .365 IN 1957. TOPPED AL IN WALKS FIVE YEARS AND IN RUNS

And there hasn't been.

SCORED SIX SEASONS. VOTED MOST VALUABLE PLAYER 1956—57—62. NAMED ON 20 AL ALL STAR TEAMS. SET WORLD SERIES RECORDS FOR HOMES: 18; RUNS: 42; RUNS BATTED IN: 40; TOTAL BASES: 123 AND BASES ON BALLS: 43

When Kuhn finished Mantle moved to the microphone.

He made a warm and wonderful talk, kidding himself about striking out so much, reminiscing about being named for Mickey Cochrane, talking about his father's dedication and encouragement. He spoke of his start in baseball and about his appreciation of Casey Stengel's support.

Stengel stood by, beaming at his boy. A little over a year later he would be dead, but today he was here to see and enjoy the success of one of his protégés.

Mantle got the biggest laugh when he told about his chicken business.

"Merlyn doesn't want me to tell this," he said to the rapt audience, "but I'm goin' to tell it anyway. I made up the slogan for our chicken and I like it, whether we use it or not: 'To get a better piece of chicken, you'd have to be a rooster.' I don't know if that's what closed up our Holiday Inn or not, but we didn't do too good after that. Actually, it was a good deal."

Mantle smiled broadly as he continued his talk.

"I listened to Mr. [Bill] Terry make a talk last night, just for the Hall of Famers, and he said that he hoped we would come back. I just hope Whitey and I can live up to the expectation and what these guys stand for. I'm sure we're going to try to. Before I leave I would just like to thank everybody for coming up here. It's been a great day for all of us and I appreciate it very much."

The crowd roared their approval as he finished his talk. Mantle waved to his family, then waved again to the crowd.

He was now enshrined with all the other greats of the game—Babe Ruth, Ty Cobb, Christy Mathewson, Walter Johnson, Ted Williams, Bill Terry, and the rest.

In more than a hundred years of professional baseball, many thousands have played professional ball, but only 215 names are listed in the Hall of Fame. It is an honor so huge in sports that it has few rivals.

Mantle came to Cooperstown only that one time, for his own induction. He was always concerned that his presence would be a distraction for the small community, and that it would diminish the attention to incoming inductees.

He was promised privacy and a good game of golf if he would only return, but he never did break away for that summer weekend to be among the Hall of Fame group. Many of them traveled to that little village in upstate New York year after year. A few continued to come well into their eighties and nineties.

The rest of the 1970s was a blur for Mantle. Years later he could hardly recall any events. One banquet ran into another, one dinner seemed pretty much like the next, and one paid appearance blended in with another.

He seemed his happiest during the few weeks he spent in Florida each spring with his Yankee pals.

"I didn't do much, but I always enjoyed being there," he told me.

He would suit up in that familiar uniform number seven, sit around the Yankees clubhouse in Fort Lauderdale, kidding with Ford, Billy Martin, and other Yankees he knew. He would walk on the field unobtrusively after practice started, lean against a railing and sign a few autographs. Occasionally he would give an interview or two to local sportswriters.

He seemed, finally, after so many turbulent years, to be comfortable with the New York press—especially those of us who had covered him for most of his brilliant career. He was always in a mood to laugh when Ford was around. After Martin became the Yankees manager late in 1975, he would wait for Billy to finish his work day. The two of them would set out for a round of golf, a few drinks, and dinner together. Mantle and Martin had their favorite hangouts in Fort Lauderdale. Here they spent many a night together, reliving the old days and sharing wonderful memories.

"I wish I could get Mick to travel with us all year," Martin told me. "It would be good for him to keep busy, and it would be good for me to have him around. I can't get him to do it. Mick has a million things to do. The trouble is, he doesn't have one thing to do."

Each year Mantle returned home to Dallas after his Fort Lauderdale fling, got back on the golf course, and made his appearances. He spoke at meetings and went to banquets and baseball signings. He was growing old with grace.

In 1981 Mickey Mantle turned fifty years old. Martin visited him that winter. They shared a golf game, and when it was over, Martin congratulated Mickey on his birthday and wished his pal well for the future.

"You know what the great thing is about turning fifty?" Martin asked Mickey. "You can't die young anymore."

Mantle Redux

A nostalgia craze exploded in America. In the late 1970s and accelerating in the 1980s the focus was on Mickey Mantle, Ted Williams, Willie Mays, and Joe DiMaggio. People were looking for autographs, photos, memorabilia, and public appearances of baseball's greatest heroes.

"I can make more money signing autographs for an hour than I did in a lot of years I played," Mantle told me. "I would have saved a lot more of my stuff if I knew I could turn it all into such big money."

Autograph card shows took on steam in the early 1980s. Mickey would travel from Dallas to Los Angeles for a weekend, sign a few thousand cards, catch the night plane back home, and be on the golf course the next morning at sunrise.

Yankees fans react with frenzy at the sight of heroes Mickey Mantle and Joe Dimaggio (in cart behind Mantle) on Old Timers Day 1969, Mantle's first appearance at Yankee Stadium as a retired ballplayer.

Mickey connects in his first at-bat as an old-timer.

Old-Timers Day 1973. (Above and below)

He was away from home almost every weekend—traveling to Los Angeles, New York, Chicago, Boston, Cleveland, or Detroit. He made the rounds of every major city in America, signing autographs, playing golf in local tournaments, and spending evenings with other retired players in hotel bars. He traveled endlessly, drinking heavily, laughing as he signed his name. He was finally a big financial success.

Early in 1983 another deal surfaced that would earn Mickey Mantle $100,000 a year, just for being Mickey Mantle. It was basically what he was doing for a living now—just being himself among mesmerized fans.

A hotel in Atlantic City, Bally's Park Place, had hired Willie Mays to be a greeter and golfer and to publicize the name of the establishment. The owners could brag about their connection to stardom.

Baseball Commissioner Bowie Kuhn responded by banning Mays from the game.

Mays had had a contract with the New York Mets that paid him $50,000 a year for promotional appearances. It was a sweetheart deal given to him by Mets owner Joan Whitney Payson in 1972 when he joined the team after his playing days with the San Francisco Giants ended.

But new Mets owners Fred Wilpon and Nelson Doubleday were not interested in extending the deal with Mays. Mays soon decided to accept the Bally proposal for $100,000 a year.

A few months later, Mantle was contacted by Bill Dougall, who had been the general manager of the Sahara Hotel in Las Vegas. Former Yankees owner Del Webb owned the Sahara, and Mantle had many a pleasant stay there, on the house.

Dougall had switched to managing the Claridge in Atlantic City, and he contacted Mantle to offer him the same deal Mays had at Bally. Mantle would be making $100,000 a year for about a dozen appearances, playing a little golf with the high rollers, and taking a stroll in his tuxedo through the casino. He could sign an autograph now and then and give a few friendly waves to the prettiest girls. No heavy lifting.

Mantle quickly accepted.

Bowie Kuhn quickly responded with a ban.

It was more psychological than pragmatic. Mantle wasn't really in baseball any more. His weeks at spring training with the Yankees and Old Timer's Day appearances were really his only connection with the game.

He missed out on Old Timer's Day in 1983 and 1984. In 1985 new Baseball Commissioner Peter Ueberroth lifted the ban. He understood the impact of names like Mays and Mantle on the game.

Now Mantle could return to baseball and also keep his job at the casino. He soon gave up the casino job, though, as card shows around the country took more and more of his free time.

Another nostalgic invention put Mantle back in the lineup in 1986. A new phenomenon, the baseball fantasy camp, was showing amazing growth.

Chicago Cubs catcher Randy Hundley, who had been a major leaguer in the 1960s and 1970s, had come up with the idea of reuniting his teammates on the Cubs for two weeks in an adult baseball camp.

Ernie Banks, Hundley, Ron Santo, Billy Williams, Ferguson Jenkins, Don Kissinger, and several other players on the 1969 Chicago team gathered once again in Arizona. This team, led by Leo Durocher, had been caught and passed in the final weeks of the season by the Mets, who won the pennant and then went on to win their first World Series.

Civilians willing to pay $1500 could spend two weeks in the Chicago Cubs training camp at Mesa, Arizona, getting baseball instruction, before a final championship game against the retired big leaguers.

That first fantasy camp was packed with over one hundred men from the ages of thirty-five to sixty-five, all eager to rub elbows with their heroes.

The Yankees knew a good thing when they saw it. The following spring Mickey Mantle, Whitey Ford, Moose Skowron, Hank Bauer, Gene Woodling, Tom Tresh, Jake Gibbs, and Hector Lopez were united at a Yankee Fantasy Camp in Fort Lauderdale, Florida.

Mantle was back in his familiar uniform number seven. He would take a few swings for fun, then stand around the batting cage, chatting. The salary wasn't much—maybe $5000 at best—but the atmosphere was almost equal to the springs he remembered thirty-five years earlier.

Mickey never really gave batting instruction. He just kidded with the campers. He acted as if they really were teammates. The banter was about the same as it had been around Yankee batting cages over the years.

Camper Steve Pilchen, a corrections officer from Davenport, Iowa, was built like a fire hydrant. He also had a great sense of humor and an appealing personality. Mantle immediately adopted him as one of his favorites.

"Hey, Pilch, where did you get that gut, in a pillow store?" he would ask.

"Nah, I just eat a lot," Pilchen said.

"You mean always."

"Ah, Mick, c'mon. It didn't hurt Babe Ruth."

"Yeah, but he could play," Mantle retorted.

The idea that Pilchen could banter with Mickey Mantle on the field,

Old-Timers Day 1974 (from left): Willie Mays, Joe Dimaggio, Casey Stengel, Mickey Mantle, Whitey Ford.

buy him a beer at night in the hotel bar, and stand around while Mick exchanged kidding remarks with his former teammates was overwhelming. The campers all ate together in the same dining room, exchanging stories. This was a thrill that would last a lifetime.

For $1500 to $2000 ($3000 as the camp popularity grew), civilians, many of them emotional Yankee fans, could be in the same orbit with these legendary baseball heroes.

You could compare this to the three remaining Beatles running a summer camp in Liverpool, playing music, getting high, romancing the girls, and sharing it all with fans.

Many of the participants considered these fantasy camps the highlight of their lives. Quite a few of them returned year after year on their vacations to mingle with their heroes, basking in the glow of reflected glory.

Eventually, Mantle and Ford established their own fantasy camp in Fort Lauderdale. It later broke up after some complicated business dealings handled by intermediaries which put a strain on their 40-year friendship.

The Atlantic City adventure, autograph card shows, the fantasy camps, appearances at spring training, Old Timer's Days, and banquets brought Mantle greater fame than he had experienced as a player.

He seemed to be everywhere in the middle 1980s. He pursued golf tournaments with a passion. Often these were for charity, and he received no expense money. He was doing so well now that he could afford to attend these charity events without any payment.

Now when I ran into him at a banquet, a golf tournament, or a public appearance, he seemed happier than he had been in years. The lines in his face were deepening now, his jawline not quite so firm, and his mid-section was a little thicker. But he was still strong and handsome, not quite the lithe Mickey Mantle of the 1950s and 1960s, but not an embarrassing old-timer either.

His fame in the middle 1980s had grown so great, partially due to the nostalgia craze, that he was now making paid public appearances at weddings, conventions, and bar mitzvahs. For the right money, ten or fifteen thousand dollars, a wealthy father could present Mantle at the cocktail hour of a treasured event.

There are dozens of proud fathers and starry-eyed sons who have home movies and snapshots of Mantle in a yarmulke at their bar mitzvah.

Early in 1987 Mickey Mantle received a phone call that was to enhance his life in New York.

Since the middle 1950s, Mantle had stayed in Manhattan at the St. Moritz Hotel on Central Park South. He was familiar with the area. It was easy for him to get a cab to the Stadium for games. At night he could walk to Toots Shor's restaurant on Fifty-Second Street.

Adjacent to the hotel was a small watering hole, a relic of the days of Prohibition, Harry's Bar. It was dark and intimate, a comfortable hangout for Mantle, his Yankee teammates, and friends. Now Harry's Bar was closing. The good times were over.

Meanwhile, two young men, Bill Liederman and John Lowy, were running a successful cooking school in Manhattan. They trained chefs for jobs in New York's finest restaurants. Their business was successful, but the two owners yearned for more hands-on action. They wanted a restaurant of their own.

Liederman had been an outstanding high-school and college athlete. He had always been a big fan of the Yankees. Like many youngsters, he

Mickey crosses the plate after homering against old teammate Whitey Ford in a 1975 Old Timers Day game.

had dreamed of someday playing for the Yankees, but had to settle instead for wearing a Yankee cap as he played in tough softball leagues in Central Park.

"We had this idea," he said one day in 1995, "that we could open a successful sports restaurant in New York. We were sports fans ourselves and we thought we could attract a sports crowd with good food, a good location and the right sports name."

They searched around Manhattan for a site. Finally they heard about Harry's Bar. The location was good—Central Park South next to the St. Moritz Hotel. The lease for the site was obtainable.

They examined the restaurant, looked over the neighborhood, and discussed the figures with real estate people and lawyers. They took an option on the place.

All they needed now was a name.

"I kept thinking we could make a big hit with good food, but we also needed a big name to draw in customers," Liederman said

But which name? Who was the most recognizable athlete in America and New York? Who was the most identifiable person, someone who had been around the city over many years?

"It just popped into my head: Mickey Mantle. I couldn't imagine that it was possible to get him in on the deal, but I decided to try," Liederman said.

Liederman had a friend named Larry Meli, an executive producer for SportsChannel, the nationally known cable television network.

Meli had hired Mantle to make some appearances for special baseball events on SportsChannel. Mickey had always been fun to have around. He laughed a lot, enjoyed a drink with the boys after the production meetings, and never played the big shot.

Meli expected to speak to Mantle about some SportsChannel business in a few days. He would mention Liederman's idea to Mantle and get back to Liederman after their talk.

Within a few days, Meli called back to say that Mickey would be in town on business and suggested that Liederman pick a place where he could meet with them.

Liederman's brother David owned a restaurant in Manhattan called Chez Louie, a comfortable, quiet, unpretentious place on the upper east side of Manhattan. Liederman called Meli and suggested his brother's restaurant—at Mantle's convenience. Meli called the St. Moritz to set the date up.

"This was about as nervous as I have ever been," recalled Liederman. "The very idea of building a restaurant from scratch is enough pressure. The idea that it could possibly have Mickey Mantle's name and Mickey himself as a part of it was just too much."

The meeting was set up at Chez Louie's on a cold February in 1987. At six o'clock Liederman and his partner, Lowy, arrived at the restaurant. Their meeting was scheduled for seven o'clock. David Liederman had moved a table into a quiet corner of the restaurant, away from the other dinner guests that evening.

Liederman and Lowy sat at the table, with Liederman so nervous he remembered the shirt under his jacket being drenched with sweat. The clock ticked away as the two partners carefully went over their pitch. It was almost seven o'clock.

A cab pulled up in front of the restaurant, and Mickey Mantle walked through the front door. David Liederman greeted him, showing him to the back table where his brother and Lowy were waiting apprehensively.

"What I remember most about that meeting," said Liederman, a trim man who stands six feet, one inch tall, "was that Mickey was shorter than I was. I couldn't believe that. I had watched him all these years. He was the greatest Yankee hero of all time to me. I thought he would be huge, just huge. He was an average sized guy."

David Liederman brought drinks all around. Mickey sat quietly as Liederman and Lowy did the talking.

"We told him our concept for this restaurant, that we had been considering it and working on the idea for months. We wanted a sports bar and restaurant, to be called Mickey Mantle's. We envisioned it as a fun place where kids could come in, buy a hamburger and take swings in a batting cage. There would be basketball hoops for guys to shoot at, and games on video. There would be walls full of pictures of players—Mickey and his teammates. Mickey and Billy, Mickey with Whitey and some other great stars. We saw it as a friendly, noisy young people's place.

"I don't want any of that crap," said Mantle.

"I just sat there, stunned," Liederman recalls. "I thought we had made a great pitch. He was paying attention, listening to everything we said, and seemed to be reasonably excited at the prospect of a restaurant with his name on Central Park South, right in the heart of Manhattan. Then he shoots it down with one quick remark. My stomach just dropped. I felt terrible."

Mantle had traveled with the Yankees to most of the major cities in America. What National League cities he had missed while playing he had visited for card shows, golf tournaments, banquets, public appearances, and bar mitzvahs. It was a rare restaurant with a bar that he had missed. He knew the subject of restaurants well.

Mantle looked Liederman and Lowy straight in the eye. He wasn't shooting down the restaurant idea—just the theme they had proposed.

"What I want is a restaurant where people my age [Mantle was fifty-five at the time] can come in, have a great dinner, have a couple of drinks. A quiet place where they can meet their friends, have a few laughs after work and go home feeling great. What I want is another Toots Shor's—a place that has a lot of companionship, guys hanging out together, meeting and laughing and talking there. Sort of a clubhouse away from the clubhouse."

Liederman and Lowy quickly agreed. It was what they wanted all along—another Toots Shor's, an adult hangout and club where successful businessmen could bring clients, their girl friends, or both. It would be a pleasant place with a sports atmosphere, and there would be no games, video machines, or kids shooting baskets.

Liederman and Lowy agreed immediately. They went back to their restaurant architect and restructured their design.

"It worked beautifully," said Lowy late in 1995. "We wanted rooms that were well lit, with wood paneling, a look that would be attractive and comfortable for a sports crowd."

It was to be somewhat upscale, with some elegant art works by renowned artists, available for purchase. In the front, expensive ties with baseball themes were displayed in the case near the cashier. If you didn't mind spending $50 for a tie, you could buy something very nice indeed.

The deal worked out beautifully. Mantle was given 7 percent of the profits of the restaurant in exchange for the use of his name. He was also expected to show up about a dozen times a year.

"We never wrote that into the contract," said Liederman. "Mick told us that if he liked the place and felt comfortable with it, he would be here a lot. If he didn't like it, or was embarrassed, he would never show up."

The restaurant, Mickey Mantle's, opened to a huge crowd on February 5, 1988.

Several of Mickey's old teammates—Whitey Ford, Hank Bauer, Billy Martin, and Moose Skowron—showed up for the event. Mantle greeted his friends, spoke warmly to strangers, signed autographs, drank some vodka, ate a bit of chicken steak, told great stories, gave television, radio, and print interviews, and enjoyed himself thoroughly.

Here was a proud successor to the famed Toots Shor's restaurant.

Mantle's became *the* place to be for all athletes in New York. Baseball, football, hockey, and tennis players hung out at the restaurant. There was always action at the bar and good food at the tables.

Mantle had his own reserved table in the rear of the restaurant and would show up whenever he was in New York. On occasion he was there for twenty or thirty days in a row.

He never missed visiting the restaurant on Old Timer's weekend with his teammates, or when there was any other Yankee special event. He made television appearances from the restaurant, hosted private parties, and appeared at dozens of press conferences. The restaurant was a huge success.

"When he was in town he would call before he came over," said Liederman. "That was to make sure I hadn't given his table away because we were packed. When he came in, he would greet all the fans at the bar, sign autographs, and then go to his table. He enjoyed spending the night there."

At the end of the evening, he didn't have far to go—upstairs to his hotel apartment at the St. Moritz.

"When he was here there was always so much excitement in the room. He couldn't have been nicer to people," said Liederman.

The restaurateur remembered one night when he brought his 86-year-old cousin Hilda Danzig to the restaurant for the first time. She was so proud of her young cousin's success as the owner of a popular New York eatery, especially one connected with the name of Mickey Mantle.

"I brought Mickey over to say hello to Hilda. He was really kind to her," said Liederman. "She looked up at him and said how happy she was to meet him. Then she told him, 'You've always been my favorite Brooklyn Dodger.' Mickey just leaned over, gave her a big kiss and told her how much he enjoyed playing baseball all those years for the Brooklyn Dodgers."

Liederman worked hard to make the restaurant popular in the food department, too. He put some exotic dishes on the menu. They featured grilled swordfish steak; herb roasted breast of chicken with white beans; penne pasta with chicken, shrimp, spinach, and roasted red peppers; and linguine with seared shrimp.

"We also put some items on the menu in a boxed and highlighted form to play them up, food like chicken fried steak which Mickey liked, hickory smoked baby back ribs, roasted breast of chicken and a dish called lobster ravioli with grilled shrimp which Mickey never tasted," Liederman said.

The boxed items were labeled "Mickey's Favorites" on the menu, and fans being fans, these items were heavy favorites.

"One day a kid was in the restaurant with his father for dinner. He was maybe thirteen or fourteen. He came up to Mickey holding the menu. 'Mr. Mantle, do you really like the lobster ravioli?' Without batting an eye Mickey said, 'Kid, I grew up eating that stuff.' It was a priceless moment," said Liederman.

A lot of families come to Mickey Mantle's. One night a Little League team that had won their neighborhood championship was being treated to dinner there. They were all wearing cut-down Yankee uniforms. While the young athletes dined off the menu with the chicken, steak, and ravioli featured at $16.95, $18.95 and $19.95, Mantle watched the team's coach squirm.

"Mick came over to me and said that we were going to have to get cheaper items for the kids. Then he walked over to the table, said he was honored the Little Leaguers chose his restaurant for their dinner, and that they were to be his guests that night. 'Give me the bill,' he told the waiter. He paid their check and the next day we worked out a less expensive menu for kids," said Liederman.

On the huge menu with a painting by Burton Silverman of the young Mantle at Yankee Stadium's dugout steps on the cover, there is now a "Little League Menu" featuring hamburgers, macaroni and cheese, and spaghetti and meatballs—all are under eight dollars.

"These items are really popular with the kids and their parents. They're good and they're inexpensive," Liederman says. "Mickey never forgot what it was like as a kid not to have any money."

Unlike many restaurants in the country that are supposed to be owned by sports stars, Mickey Mantle's was part of his business domain and a wonderfully happy hangout for him.

"I'm not a religious person," said Liederman, "but the presence of Mickey just hangs over this place. You can feel it. You can see it."

Photos and paintings of Mantle line the walls. An etching of Yankee Stadium shows the young Mantle driving a ball right-handed over the left center field wall. Copies of his Yankee uniforms through the years are displayed in the front of the restaurant in glass cases.

"I went to Mickey's funeral in Dallas," Liederman said. " I felt as though a part of me had died with him. It was an eerie feeling."

For several weeks after Mantle's death in August of 1995, business declined. People seemed to be staying away almost as a sign of respect.

"Then things went back to normal," Liederman said. "The laughter, the fraternity, the joy of the place as it was when Mickey was here, it all came back."

Liederman looked over at one of the Yankee uniform shirts behind the glass in the case. It was a traveling Yankee uniform with the name sewn into the lower flap. On the back could be seen the number seven.

"You know," said Liederman, "in some strange way I think people understand all this when they come in here—about Mickey's presence and all, about the fact that nothing really has changed. Mickey will always be a part of this place." He looked out over the crowded bar and at the diners eating their chicken, steak, and ribs. "People told me this after Mickey died and I really didn't believe it at first. I do now. Mickey is like Elvis and John Lennon, bigger in death than he ever was in life."

Maybe those famous persons who die before their time or end in a sad or violent way do live on with even greater recognition. Think of

Marilyn Monroe, James Dean, John F. Kennedy, Abraham Lincoln, Martin Luther King, Bobby Kennedy, and Mickey Mantle.

"I miss him," said Liederman. "I guess I always will."

◆◆◆

After Liederman opened the restaurant and became a close friend of Mantle's, he began attending the Mantle and Ford fantasy camp each year.

"I'm a catcher and I could still crouch," said Liederman. "Those games were fun. Mickey would always take a swing and most of the time he would hit it out."

One time Billy Martin, between jobs, showed up at the camp. He suited up with Mantle and Ford. It was just like old times for the three friends.

Martin also had an interest in a Manhattan store, Billy Martin's Western Shop on Madison Avenue in Manhattan. Unlike Mantle's, it was not a hangout, and Martin only went there once or twice a year.

Martin liked to kid Mantle about having a business before Mickey did in Manhattan. He suggested that his shop carried the kind of western clothes that would make cowboys out of all New Yorkers.

"Pardner, you'll see everyone wearing Billy Martin's western clothes down every street in Manhattan before too long," Martin boasted.

"Only if *you* buy it all," Mantle joked.

In the early 1980s Mantle and Martin often met at golf tournaments, at baseball banquets, and once in a while on a hunting trip. Mostly they hunted for laughs and a few beers. Relationships between ballplayers are usually quite tenuous, but this was one where there was a terrific continuing attachment. No matter how many jobs Martin lost, no matter how many baseball fights on and off the field he got involved in, no matter how many times George Steinbrenner humbled Martin and abused him, Mantle was never far off, with a quip.

Their relationship had begun as teammates in 1951, and it remained strong for the rest of their lives.

On Christmas Day, 1989, the great friendship ended.

Billy Martin was vacationing in Johnson City, New York, on a farm he had bought a year earlier with his new wife, Jill. It was his fourth try at marriage.

He was depressed and restless, as he almost always was when he was away from baseball. At the age of sixty-one, he recognized that he might just have blown his last baseball job. As day after day passed without a call from any baseball owner, he grew sadder. He called Mantle a few days before Christmas at his Dallas home. Mickey was traveling. Merlyn was never particularly fond of Billy. She knew he encouraged Mickey's drinking and absences from home, but she did promise to have Mickey call as soon as she heard from him.

Martin invited a friend from Detroit, William Reedy, to join him for Christmas dinner at his upstate New York home. His friend accepted.

Reedy flew in the day before Christmas. They sat around the house, talking baseball and enjoying the out-of-doors. They were waiting for the Christmas celebration Billy's wife was preparing.

Shortly after noon on Christmas Day, Billy and his pal decided they would take a little ride to the village tavern for a couple of drinks before dinner. It was a guy thing. No need to stay in the house waiting while the turkey was cooking.

Late in the afternoon, they finally decided to head back home to Billy's farm.

The story the 53-year-old Reedy later told police was a little muddled. It was never made clear exactly who was driving the vehicle when it skidded on an icy curve about one hundred yards from the entrance to Billy's farm.

The car crashed through a stone barrier, rolled over several times, and came to rest on its side about three hundred feet from the road.

It was 5:45 in the afternoon on Christmas Day.

By the time the ambulance was called and Billy was taken to nearby Wilson Memorial Hospital in Fenton, New York, there was little hope. His young wife, Jill, was at his side when doctors at the hospital pronounced Billy Martin dead at seven o'clock that evening.

Broome County Sheriff Anthony Ruffo investigated the accident. He charged Reedy with driving while intoxicated. Police could never confirm whether Reedy was driving the car or whether Martin had been driving.

For many months, rumors persisted that Martin, in fact, was the driver and that Reedy had taken the blame for his pal to protect him.

It hardly mattered. A man who had been the center of so many episodes in so many bars throughout his playing and his managerial career was a good bet to end up this way. No one could be terribly surprised.

With great sadness, Mickey Mantle attended Billy Martin's funeral in New York. He did not speak. He sat silently between Yankee owner George Steinbrenner and former president Richard Nixon. The pain of losing one of his closest friends was great.

Just ten years earlier the Yankees had been involved in the funeral of their team captain, catcher Thurman Munson. Munson had crashed his private plane while practicing takeoffs and landings at the Canton-Akron Airport.

Munson died almost immediately when his plane ignited with fuel and smoke filled the cabin. Two friends of Munson, David Hall and Jerry Anderson, were in the plane, a Cessna Citation twin engine, when it crashed. Hall suffered severe burns in the crash. Anderson suffered broken ribs. Both men soon recovered.

Munson was only thirty-two years old.

Billy Martin, fishing on a New Jersey lake with his son, Billy Joe, was called on a ship-to-shore phone. Martin was instructed to call Steinbrenner immediately. When he reached Steinbrenner from a nearby harbor shop, the Yankee owner told him, "We have just gotten some terrible news. Thurman has been killed in a crash."

No man seemed to suffer more at Munson's funeral in Akron than Billy Martin. He cried constantly through the funeral. Photographs of his tear-stained face filled the New York papers the following day.

Now it was the other members of the Yankees family who were crying at the death of Martin.

There is something emotionally wrenching for all who know an athlete when they consider his loss. These are men who have provided wonderful entertainment. It is their youthful accomplishments that we all remember. No matter when they go or how they go, it is perceived as too difficult, too painful, too soon.

Yankee owner George Steinbrenner had helped arrange for a magnificent funeral in Akron for his catcher and Yankee captain. He did the same for Billy Martin in Manhattan at St. Patrick's Cathedral.

John Cardinal O'Connor was the celebrant at the mass for Billy. Local politicians, baseball executives, civic leaders, teammates, and friends addressed a huge crowd in the historic church.

When the ceremony was over, on a crisp winter afternoon in December, some old Yankees stood on a corner of Fifth Avenue reliving their youth, telling stories about Billy and Mickey. They all agreed that Billy had lasted a lot longer than any of them thought he would. They all thought about Mickey and Whitey, who were moving into their late fifties.

There were not many tears that afternoon. Billy Martin had lived a hard life and experienced a hard death. His old Yankee pals agreed that his life style had done Billy Martin in, as surely as the slippery, icy road he died on.

Mickey in 1985 with old pals Billy Martin and Mel Allen.

A Brave Farewell

Broadcaster Bob Costas liked to tell a story on the air about his Mickey Mantle baseball card. He had come across the treasured card when he was seven or eight and kept it on his night table at home. When he was older, he transferred it to his wallet where he would produce it on demand.

For many years in the 1980s and 1990s, friends, fans, strangers, the curious approached him at airports, restaurants, and ballparks.

"Let's see if you really got it," they would say.

He would reach down in his back pocket and pull out his wallet. Slowly, he would slide the Mickey Mantle 1957 Topps baseball card from its plastic cover and show it off.

"It got so that I could not leave the house without checking for my Mickey Mantle in the wallet," Costas said in 1995, "the way guys check for their car license before they take a trip."

By the early 1990s, that shy, unassuming country boy from

Oklahoma, that unassuming, heroic baseball star and mythic figure of American lore, got the message.

He finally knew, finally recognized and appreciated, his own stature in American life.

It didn't change him one whit. He wouldn't tolerate frauds or phonies in his life. It just wasn't his style.

As he came to recognize the scope of his fame, his significance on the American scene, his own immortality, he was more tolerant of the hero-worshipping attitude of fans.

What he had considered silly, weak, and even childish he now understood on an emotional level. People surrounded him at card shows, screamed his name at banquets, lined up for hours at book signings. They inundated him with uncontrolled affection.

There is no way to explain what happened in the late 1980s and 1990s. There was an incredible bonding between the famous and their fans. For Mantle, it included, not only middle-aged men who had watched him for years in stadiums around the country, but women of every age, children, politicians, theater people, blue-collar workers—Americans from all walks of life.

In 1990 Mantle collapsed on a plane after a long flight and was rushed to a hospital. At the time, exhaustion was the excuse given by friends of the family. They blamed his nonstop schedule and his constant traveling to card shows, banquets, and book appearances.

In truth, the family knew he was breaking down. The hard life was costing him dearly.

Letters poured into the hospital in Dallas where he lay recovering from a battery of tests. The sheer number of letters overwhelmed him. The intensity of their emotion for him surprised him still.

Mickey and Merlyn Mantle had four sons—Mickey Jr., Danny, Billy, and David. By the early 1990s, these boys were their father's buddies. They could be found hanging out in Dallas bars late into the night, drinking too much, and in the process damaging both themselves and their families.

It was as though Mantle was struggling to recapture the fraternalism of his youth and the joyous connection he had shared with his teammates. He still loved the macho life style of outdrinking and outpartying everyone around him.

By this time, Merlyn and Mickey were no longer living together. Mickey was staying with his son David on those rare occasions when he was in Dallas, while Merlyn still lived in their big home located on a cul-de-sac in Dallas.

Mickey's choked up as Roger Maris and he are honored in mid 1985 at Yankee Stadium.

At the age of nineteen, Billy Mantle was diagnosed with Hodgkin's disease. Hodgkin's is a malignant, progressive disease, always fatal in the Mantle family. No one knows its causes or origins. It is marked by enlargement of the lymph nodes, spleen, and liver. This was the disease that had killed Mickey's father, his grandfather, and two uncles—all before they were forty years old. Now Billy Mantle, the child who had been named after Billy Martin, was to suffer the same fate. He lived with intermittent pain over the next seventeen years, dying in 1993 at the age of thirty-six.

As it turned out, 1993 was also the year that Mickey Mantle, as brave, heroic, and proud a man as ever played the game, checked himself into the Betty Ford Clinic in Rancho Mirage, California. He stayed for thirty-two days. At the clinic he wasn't a big-shot baseball player, a heroic figure, or even a famous one. He was just the man in room 202 who was fighting his own personal demons of alcoholic addiction.

I wrote him a letter when he entered the clinic, kidding him about trying to duck out of that year's Old Timer's Day because the Yankees were having such an embarrassing season. He never answered my letter. It was one of twenty thousand he received during that thirty-two day period.

Newspapers reported the phenomenal amount of mail he was receiving, which seemed to generate even more interest in Mickey's life than what he had previously accomplished, both on and off the field.

He was waging the most heroic battle of his life. Staying sober is not easy. Not for any one. This was especially true for Mickey Mantle. He was constantly in and around places where drinking was a habitual part of the scene—in country clubs after a round of golf, at banquets in fancy hotels, in the bars on the road during his travels, at the private parties he attended, and at the command performances where he earned so much just appearing as an honored guest.

"I was expected to get drunk," he once said. "That's what people wanted of me."

Now he came out of Betty Ford Clinic sober. He had won a very big battle. Each day he was better for it. Each day he was stronger.

"I remember the first time he came to the restaurant after Betty Ford," said Bill Liederman as he stood in Mickey Mantle's. "He went to the back table, just like he always had. I didn't quite know how to deal with him. He was great. He asked for a soda and he sat there with a couple of his pals. He laughed as easily as he always had. He told old stories, bouncing around the place, shaking hands with fans and signing autographs for them. He posed for pictures with kids. He was just wonderful."

The next night Mantle returned to the restaurant again, about half past nine at night. He asked the chef to get him some of his favorite chicken steak and a little salad.

"I sat with him and we just talked about some things we were planning for the restaurant," said Liederman. "There was an Arthritis Foundation benefit auction that was being hosted by David Cone." Cone had been with the Mets and still lived in Manhattan, even though he now played for Kansas City. "Mickey agreed immediately to be there," Liederman recalled.

Liederman also remembered how Mantle looked at him that night, smiled, and suddenly said, "You can't imagine how good it feels to be sober."

A few weeks later his old broadcasting pal Bob Costas got Mantle to sit for a one-hour special interview on television. Costas, who is a remarkable interviewer, led Mantle in a conversation through a mine field of subjects—his drinking, his stay at Betty Ford, his regrets concerning his less than devoted attention to his family, and his personal disappointments.

But with Costas he also relived those moments of incredible success, the joyous home runs, fraternal relationships, pennants, his own personal heroism in the face of constant injury. People were reminded of his magnificent accomplishments.

What came through the television screen was his honesty, his remarkable love for life, his appreciation of his God-given skills, his incredibly self-deprecating humor. Rarely has there been as great a baseball player who dealt with his success and his career as modestly as Mantle.

He returned to his usual routine, but without the booze. He went to the card shows, stuffing huge wads of cash into his pockets, and flew off to the next golf tournament.

Late in 1994 the New York chapter of the Baseball Writers discussed and debated its dinner potential. Baseball was in a blue-funk period with the brutal strike going on. Most were concerned that if the Baseball Writers Dinner, which had survived for seventy-five years, did not go on as usual in 1995, it might never be revived. Such was the sour disposition of the fans, and rightfully so.

Losing the dinner would be too much to bear for those who connected emotionally with this annual baseball extravaganza. We moved forward, propelled by our new award, an excuse to place the winners on the dais, the Willie, Mickey and the Duke Award.

With his most recent struggles uppermost in the mind of everyone, Mickey's arrival at the dinner sent an electric charge through the VIP reception room. There was an enormous emotional outburst through the hotel ballroom later on when he appeared for dinner.

The entire evening worked wonderfully.

We closed the night at Mickey Mantle's restaurant, laughing over old times and looking ahead to new ones. Mickey kidded me about coming to another Yankee Fantasy Camp in my sixties, as I had in my fifties.

"I'll tell all my pitchers to knock you on your ass, where you belong," he said.

He still had the same short haircut I always remembered, but his hair was a little gray around the edges. He was bulkier than he had been when we both were young, but he was not as heavy as many former athletes his age. His voice was the same. The Oklahoma twang rang out as distinctively as it ever had.

For the first time, I had brought my 25-year-old son Ted to the dinner. He posed for a picture with Mickey, Duke, and Willie. It was an

Yankee Hall of Famers are honored at a 1987
Old Timers Game (from second from left):
Enos Slaughter, Johnny Mize, Lefty Gomez,
Whitey Ford, Mickey Mantle, Joe Dimaggio,
Catfish Hunter.

honor he could hardly begin to comprehend. Baseball had never been his thing. He would have been more excited if I could have gotten him together with Billy Joel.

His mother Janet, his sister Jennifer and her husband Tom, and their daughter Amanda were all duly impressed. When friends came to Ted's Manhattan apartment, they were dazzled by his great good luck. The photograph hangs alone on a wall where all can see and appreciate it.

When I visited my son in the weeks following the dinner and looked at the picture, I couldn't help but recall how I had shyly asked Mickey to pose with me some thirty years earlier. I had never been one of those sportswriters who asked for a photograph with every baseball star, but Mickey was something else. Back in the early 1960s, I had understood his impact. It hadn't taken long to realize that years later he would be lionized as one of a handful of the game's immortals. I wanted to have a picture of myself with Mickey, a fond memory for myself, and to show my grandchild.

And so I have.

We both went back to our chores. I wrote. Mickey played golf.

Then one day, in early June of 1995, a wire service story caught my eye. I saw that Mickey, complaining of severe stomach pain, had checked himself into a Dallas hospital.

Doctors in Dallas revealed that he had a cancerous liver. He needed a transplant, and he was so badly off that without one he would die within days.

It was sad news, but hardly surprising.

I watched, listening for reports about Mantle, sending him a couple of photographs of himself with Willie Mays and Duke Snider from the Baseball Writers Dinner to cheer him up. I talked about him on radio and television, wondering about the reaction around the country if he didn't survive.

Very quickly a donor was found, with a match to replace Mickey's diseased liver.

On June 8, 1995, he was operated on. The procedure was complicated but successful. Doctors reported that the new liver was functioning well. There were no signs of rejection.

But along with the surgery and the new liver, there was controversy. Mantle had been operated on less than a day after the announcement of his need for a new liver. Was there favoritism? Doctors denied it. Many people didn't care. This was Mickey Mantle. Shouldn't doctors give him an edge? He had entertained millions. Didn't he deserve a favor? The doctors said the match had been made by computers. I wanted to believe them. I didn't care if it was true.

Within a few days he was improving, moving around well. In ten days he was at home again, with Merlyn and his boys caring for him lovingly.

He held a press conference at the hospital, admitted his mistakes in lifestyle, and admonishing the country not to follow his past examples, boozing it up as he had. He advised others to live a life of moderation and thanked the anonymous donor for the liver that had saved his life. Even here he was able to use his star status, urging the public to sign donor cards and to give life to others. The number of those who did so went up dramatically due to his high visibility. The public recognized the value of his request. They could help, too, in the future.

He handled his illness and his recovery with calm, dignity, and bravery.

Then came a shocking surprise. It was an announcement no doctor likes to make. The cancer, they now found, had spread to other organs. Mickey Mantle, new liver and all, hadn't much longer to live.

This time it was clear. He was gone.

With sadness I wrote my column for the Gannett Suburban Newspapers in Westchester County of New York, the paper I work for now after many years at the *New York Post*. While I suggested that it was natural to feel sorrow, as all New Yorkers certainly would, I wanted to be sure that no one felt pity for Mickey. "He lived the life he chose," I wrote. This was my deepest emotion about him. He had been a heck of a hero. That is enough for any life, no matter how it ends. The column ran on August 12, 1995.

The next day Mickey Mantle was gone.

Tributes filled the pages of newspapers, resonated on television, filled hours of radio talk programs. Former teammates and complete strangers wept. The talk in offices, bars, hotels, restaurants, playgrounds, and schools was of Mickey and his deeds. Mickey Mantle. It resonated across America and around the world, in every place where fans had seen him swing a baseball bat.

The funeral was held at Lovers Lane United Methodist Church in Dallas. They rounded up the usual suspects—George Steinbrenner; Reggie Jackson; former teammates Yogi Berra, Whitey Ford, Johnny Blanchard, Moose Skowron; and Bobby Murcer, his old Oklahoma pal who, aside from the family, had been the major presence at Thurman Munson's funeral sixteen years earlier. Billy Crystal was there, as was New York Governor George Pataki.

More important than all of them were the fans. Guys from the neighborhood, from the Bronx, who happened to be in Dallas or who traveled there, because they had to be a part of this ending too.

"I saw him as a rookie," said Stephen Tambone, age seventy-two, who had grown up in the Bronx. Tambone lives in Sanger, Texas, outside of Dallas now, but he remembered. "I used to go to the Stadium every day. I wanted to say good-bye to him."

Dallas native Randy Mayeux, forty-four, told a reporter, "I remember Mantle from my childhood. I realized when I woke up this morning, I had to come."

Eight-year-old Augie Furst of Dallas sat on a curb outside the church with her five-year-old brother, Manie. Augie wore a Yankee cap and jersey. Manie wore a white tee shirt with the number seven scrawled on the back in magic marker.

They learned about Mickey from their dad, they told the reporter.

"I think he was good," said Augie "It makes me kind of sad."

On computers, hackers messaged each other about Mantle. They shared photos on screens, Mantle baseball stats, old comments from opposing pitchers or teammates, using modern technology to bring their hero to life.

The service for Mantle was tasteful, and surprisingly upbeat. The family showed a brave face. Celebrity players who turned out were quiet and dignified, remembering their friend.

It was *the* television event of the day. Bobby Richardson, as he had promised Mantle years earlier, gave the eulogy. His sermon was touching. Local ministers who spoke were poignant. Bob Costas, great Mantle fan and friend, was warm and wonderful as he reminisced. He talked of Mickey's career, how brilliant it was. He spoke about how Mickey had handled the pressures and the pain through all his years, and how his finest inning, his final inning, during his illness, may well have been his brightest and his bravest.

He finished his eulogy by saying, "It brings to mind a story Mickey liked to tell on himself. Maybe some of you have heard it. He pictured himself at the pearly gates, met by St. Peter who shook his head and said, 'Mick, we checked the record. We know some of what went on. Sorry we can't let you in. But before you go, God wants to know if you'd sign these six dozen baseballs.'

"Well, there were days when Mickey Mantle was so darn good that we kids would bet that even God would want his autograph.

"I just hope God has a place for him where he can run again, where

Mickey and ex-Yankee pitching sensation Ron Guidry at Mickey Mantle's Restaurant in New York City, 1990

The generation of Yankees who succeeded Mantle pose with him at his restaurant in 1991 (from left): Mantle, Harding Peterson (assistant Yankee General Manager), Bucky Dent, Willie Randolph, George Steinbrenner, and Ron Guidry.

he can play practical jokes on his teammates and smile that boyish smile, 'cause God knows no one's perfect. And God knows there's something special about heroes.

"So long, Mick. Thanks."

There was hardly a dry eye in the audience when Costas finished. Millions of people across America sat weeping before their television sets.

For days afterwards his old teammates were besieged by friends and strangers alike, asked to recall his deeds, to talk about those home runs he hit, those catches he made, those moments of emotional inspiration he provided just by showing up in the lineup when others in the same state of health would never have considered it.

He had touched so many lives in so many ways. His name, his face, his deeds were imprinted in millions of minds.

I know he was not the best baseball player ever. That honor goes to Babe Ruth or Ty Cobb or Willie Mays. I know he never set records for home runs in a season, or in a lifetime. I know even his strikeout records have been passed. His World Series home run mark could be challenged by any new young slugger, and perhaps someday will be passed.

Mickey's last public appearance, the New York Writers Dinner, January 1995. Duke Snider (left), Willie Mays, and Mickey Mantle *were* New York baseball in the fifties, the era many consider baseball's finest.

I know also that he played the game as hard and as well as he could, that he lived his life fully. I will always remember his laugh, his wonderfully athletic good looks and his name, Mickey Mantle, and how it connected him to millions of fans.

I know that, if he was not the best the game ever saw, he was certainly the most loved.

THE END

Index